Johann Gottfried Herder

Twayne's World Authors Series
German Literature

TWAS 786

JOHANN GOTTFRIED HERDER
(1744–1803)

Photograph courtesy of Freies Deutsches Hochstift,
Frankfurter Goethe-Museum, Frankfurt am Main

Johann Gottfried Herder

By Wulf Koepke

Texas A&M University

Twayne Publishers
A Division of G. K. Hall & Co. • *Boston*

Johann Gottfried Herder

Wulf Koepke

Published by Twayne Publishers
A Division of G.K. Hall & Co.
70 Lincoln Street
Boston, Massachusetts 02111

Copyediting supervised by Lewis DeSimone
Book production by Elizabeth Todesco
Book design by Barbara Anderson

Typeset in 11 pt. Garamond
by Modern Graphics, Inc., Weymouth, Massachusetts

Printed on permanent/durable acid-free paper
and bound in the United States of America

Library of Congress Cataloging in Publication Data

Köpke, Wulf, 1928–
  Johann Gottfried Herder.

  (Twayne's world authors series. German literature)
  Bibliography: p. 135
  Includes index.
  1. Herder, Johann Gottfried, 1744–1803—Criticism and
interpretation. I. Title. II. Series.
PT2354.K62   1987   838'.609   84-14867
ISBN 0-8057-6634-0

Contents

About the Author

Wulf Koepke was born in Luebeck, Germany. He received his Ph.D. from the University of Freiburg after studies at Hamburg, Freiburg, and Paris. He has taught and held administrative positions in Singapore, Munich, Chicago, Houston, and Los Angeles. At present he is professor of German at Texas A&M University. His publications include *Erfolglosigkeit: Zum Frühwerk Jean Pauls* (1977), *Johann Gottfried Herder: Innovator through the Ages* (1982), *Lion Feuchtwanger* (1983), and *Deutschsprachige Exilliteratur im Kontext der Epoche 1930 bis 1960* (1984); he is coeditor of the yearbook *Exilforschung* and the author and coauthor of several textbooks. Professor Koepke has published over seventy articles and chapters in books, including on Jean Paul Richter, Herder, the period of Goethe, Thomas and Heinrich Mann, Max Frisch, Wolfgang Borchert, Hans Magnus Enzensberger, exile studies, and the methodology of foreign language teaching. Professor Koepke is one of the initiators of the Herder Study Group and has organized numerous conference panels on Herder. In November 1985, he was elected founding president of the new International Herder Society.

Preface

Johann Gottfried Herder lived from 1744 to 1803 and is remembered mainly as the mentor of the young Goethe, who was five years younger, and as a progressive thinker who formulated seminal ideas that were to be developed by others. One of the aims of this book is to show that this traditional image is far from revealing the total achievement of Herder. Indeed, it has helped to keep scholars from reading Herder's own texts, since his successors had improved so much on his original insights. This was a common view that helped to perpetuate a particular image of Herder, and that suggested that a fresh look at his work was unnecessary.

Herder has been considered the mastermind of the Sturm und Drang movement of the 1770s. Likewise, he was regarded as the chief architect of the German rebellion against Enlightenment thinking. However, scholarship of the last twenty years has radically changed the traditional view of the age of Goethe. Common features of the Enlightenment, Sturm und Drang, *Klassik,* and even romanticism are now emphasized, and the common ideas and interests of the writers and thinkers, despite many disputes and factions, were acknowledged. This was a period of transition, upheaval, even revolutionary change, and Herder was one of its typical and foremost representatives. Without undue generalization it can be said that his age formulated and propagated the ideas that were to replace the absolutistic authority of state and church in Germany. In response to a critical awareness of the limits of Enlightenment rationalism, the thinkers and writers of the age tried to find an integrative approach that granted full value to the human personality and its needs and freedom as well as to its social obligations. While the Holy Roman Empire of the German Nation and the authoritative church orthodoxies were breaking up, new ideas were emerging: freedom of opinion, free enterprise, regard for individual rights in religious and legal matters, and nationalism as self-determination of a people as opposed to rigid state structures. A new sense of religion, history, and personal freedom was emerging.

Herder was in the midst of this turbulent development. However, it would be misleading to call his views simply "progressive." Indeed, one of the major tenets of the age was its critique of the Enlightenment concept of historical progress. It perceived the dangers of individualism, as well as of social fragmentation and economic division of labor. Herder was a universalist, and his works deal with religion, society, literature, history, psychology, science, aesthetics, the arts, and education. He stubbornly clung to *Ganzheit,* to the Spinozist and Leibnizian idea of All and One *(Ein und alles, hen kai pan).* There is a counterbalancing of progressive and conservative ideas in all of the great Germans of the period—Goethe, Mozart, Karl Friedrich Schinkel, and Hegel, to name a few.

Herder's work is not only a prime example for the heroic effort to achieve a Renaissance universality and synthesis, but also for the futility of such an effort. Thus his writings became fragments, ideas, contributions for the great work that could not be written; they were seeds *(Samenkörner),* as he put it, which might or might not bear fruit. Although informed by central ideas and a central purpose, they appear rather like scattered leaves.

This appearance of Herder's oeuvre is another main reason his recognized stature and significance are in inverse proportion to the study of his works. Hans Georg Gadamer's statement of 1942, that Herder was the one among the great minds of the period of Goethe whose works were no longer read,[1] has still a good deal of validity. The only critical edition is that by Bernhard Suphan and his collaborators, published between 1877 and 1913. It is far from complete and has been criticized for its editorial practices and commentary.[2] So far the only edition of a representative choice of works for a wider audience has been published in the German Democratic Republic.[3] However, the very active Herder scholarship in the Democratic Republic—with its excellent edition of Herder's letters[4] and many other contributions—had to recur to a reprint of Rudolf Haym's monumental biography of 1877 and 1885, *Herder: Nach seinem Leben und seinen Werken dargestellt,* in order to provide a basis for scholarly work, in spite of methodological and ideological reservations.[5] Haym's book, written before most of the Suphan edition appeared, still remains the standard biography. Many short biographies are in print, of course, and the English-speaking world relies heavily on Robert T. Clark's *Herder: His Life and Thought* (1955).[6] The fact remains, however, that most Herder studies deal with specific aspects of his work, and synthesizing efforts are extremely rare. Herder himself invites such an approach. His name is mentioned in literary criticism, aesthetics, linguistics, anthropology, comparative literature, theology (especially Bible studies and comparative religion), history, education, and even geography and psychology. Naturally, each of these disciplines sees Herder from its own perspective.[7]

Most disciplines have a problem with Herder. While it seems appropriate to claim him as one of the precursors or founders, his universalist approach raises questions as to his scientific methods. In addition, his highly metaphorical style has earned Herder the reputation of being vague, although suggestive, in his pronouncements. Indeed, he is the opposite of a model for sober scientific discourse. Nor did he intend to communicate on that level. A proper understanding of his language is thus a prerequisite for an understanding of his ideas. This is not as simple as it seems, since it involves recognition of a special kind of discourse.

Historically, Herder has been too close to Goethe to be considered in his own right. The phrase "Age of Goethe" suggests the image of Goethe as the sun and all other figures as his satellites. In the case of Herder, his close personal ties with Goethe have determined the perspective. Herder's short stay in Strassburg in 1770–71 and his encounter with Goethe, their collaboration on the collection of essays *Von deutscher Art und Kunst* (1773), and Herder's works after the renewal of their friendship in 1783, notably the *Ideen zur Philosophie der Geschichte der Menschheit,* have absorbed most scholarly attention. Conversely, works written at a time of estrangement from Goethe, especially those of the last years of Herder's life, have been criticized. Generally, the problems in Herder's relationship with Goethe have been attributed to Herder's sarcasm, envy, and jealousy. This judgment not only overlooks Goethe's own difficult personality, but also ignores the real philosophical and political conflicts between these men. It is largely based on Goethe's own account of their meeting in Strassburg in *Dichtung und Wahrheit* (Poetry and Truth), where Herder's ill humor is seen as a consequence of an eye ailment. Goethe's late statements to Eckermann and others confirmed the idea that Herder had had an enormously fertile but rather chaotic mind and that he was given to negative attitudes and judgments, especially in his late years. Moreover, times had progressed. Like Klopstock, Lessing, and Wieland, Herder had been one of the writers who had prepared the great achievements of German culture. Now, however (speaking after 1825), Goethe felt, Herder's works, even the *Ideas,* had been absorbed into German culture to such a degree that one did not have to read them in order to know them.[8] That is a very dubious and dangerous compliment, and marks the beginning of the neglect of Herder's texts—which Goethe himself certainly knew most intimately.

Herder's importance for Goethe's life and work was clearly decisive, and perhaps even more pervasive than scholars usually admit. Yet, Herder's impact should not diminish Goethe's stature, and his relationship with Goethe should not blind scholars to the many other aspects of his achievement. There is a tendency to speak of Hamann and Herder, Goethe and Herder, Kant and Herder, Lessing and Herder, as if Herder could not be considered on his own. Herder became, indeed, creative through dialogue, and much of his work is a response to works with which he disagreed. He valued lasting friendship and exchange of ideas. Still, he had his own distinctive concerns, which are expressed in all of his works.

Thus, for better or worse, Herder's life and reception have been intertwined with the controversies and personal disagreements of his time. It was a distinct handicap for Herder that he sharply disagreed with Goethe's and Schiller's cultural policies after 1794, and that he considered Kant's critical philosophy fallacious and the influence of Kantianism harmful. Moreover, the early reception of Herder's work fell into the early stage of German nationalism. Herder had vigorously opposed the notion of literature as an adornment for a ruler's court, and as a game of intellectuals. Genuine literature springs from the *Volk* itself, the ethnic community that is the true cultural unit and source for creative energy. Without such social and cultural community, based on a common language, there cannot be a nation, but only artificial and power-hungry states. Herder found such genuine poetry in the Old Testament, in Homer's Greece, and in Shakespeare's England. Folk songs and other forms of folk literature preserve the spirit of a *Volk.* Goethe, Herder felt, could have been capable of creating a true German folk literature.

The nationalist movements of the nineteenth century, especially those of Eastern Europe, appropriated Herder's ideas for their own purposes. Herder had maintained, however, that a nation based on a genuine culture would be peaceful, because it would respect other nations, and that concern for humanity as a whole was more important than concern for one's own nation. No aggressive and exclusive nationalism could, in truth, claim Herder as its own. But this is what happened in a number of instances, most notoriously with the Nazi ideology. By using selected and sometimes distorted quotations, the Nazis appropriated Herder's ideas, and he emerged with a tarnished image after 1945. East German scholarship moved rather vigorously to counteract this image and redefine Herder's place in history,[9] whereas West German scholars until recently tended to ignore him.[10] There is a remarkable continuity in British Herder studies; these stress his reception of English literature and his social ideas.[11] In the United States, the repercussions of German cultural history are more evident than in Great Britain. An ongoing Herder scholarship, summarized in Clark's above-mentioned work, was interrupted after World War II and has only recently been revived.[12] No recent edition of Herder's works in English is available. The few existing translations are outdated.[13]

There is one further aspect of Herder's life and work that has caused misunderstanding. While some writers in late-eighteenth-century Germany questioned the traditional authorities, the attitude was reformist rather than revolutionary. Religion and church were a crucial battleground, both in matters of faith and in social policy. Whereas many writers and philosophers were sons of Lutheran ministers or had studied theology, few chose a career in the church, although the material prospects were good. Herder was one of those few who remained in the church. In fact, with the help of Goethe, he became the key church official for the duchy of Sachsen-Weimar. He worked tirelessly for the improvement of church administration and church services, and for a more humane spirit within the church. At the same time, his position as a *Generalsuperintendent* and court preacher was not without consequences for his writings (and not just theological works). Although Herder initially tried to separate his work as a *freier Schriftsteller*[14] from his official duties, he could not maintain this dichotomy. Works published anonymously were immediately attributed to their real author. Increasingly, he felt that there were restraints put on his writing, beyond the usual problems with censorship. Although he would never write anything against his convictions, he did not always say everything he had on his mind. Furthermore, religion remained foremost in his thoughts, and his role as a preacher and inspector of schools colored his style and his perception of his audience. These concerns were never forgotten, even in writings on aesthetics and history. Although his orthodoxy was questioned again and again, and with good reason,

Herder's affiliation with the Lutheran church separates him from most contemporary writers and from their very independent attitudes. Again, Herder's views were on the borderline of what the church could tolerate; still, the connection is crucial.

The most diverse, somewhat chaotic nature of Herder's writings, together with his peculiar style, hide the fact that Herder had some central ideas and concerns that remained with him from his student days to the end of his life. For example, he never wavered from his belief in the fundamental unity of language and thought. There is a unity, even stubborn tenacity, in Herder's writings. Following, in a Herderian spirit, the development of these central points in their historical sequence will best reveal their significance. Given the precedents, emphasis has been given to Herder's own development and achievement.

I am aware of the dangers of such a general introduction for the nonspecialist. I request the specialists to be tolerant and to be mindful of the fact that this type of basic orientation is needed and serves good purposes.

I wish to express my gratitude to Ulrich Weisstein, general editor of the series, for his guidance, suggestions, and help, and to the very able and helpful staff at G. K. Hall. My colleague Roger Crockett has given me valuable editorial assistance.

Wulf Koepke

Texas A&M University

Chronology

1783   Renews friendship with Goethe.

1784–1791   *Ideas for the Philosophy of the History of Humankind.*

1784–1797   Six collections of *Scattered Leaves.*

1787   *God: Some Conversations.*

1788–1789   Travels to Rome and Naples.

1789   Vice-president of the Weimar Consistorium. Declines offer for a professorship in Göttingen.

1793–1797   *Letters for the Advancement of Humanity.*

1794–1795   Friendship between Goethe and Schiller. Estrangement from Goethe.

1794–1798   *Christian Writings.*

1795–1796   *Terpsichore.*

1796   Jean Paul Richter's visit to Weimar and friendship with Herder.

1799   *Metacritique.*

1800   *Kalligone.*

1801   Consistorial president. Title of nobility conferred by the elector of Bavaria.

1801–1804   *Adrastaea.*

1803   Herder dies on 18 December in Weimar.

Chapter One
A Brief Biography

Johann Gottfried Herder was born on 25 August 1744 in the little town of Mohrungen (now Morag) in East Prussia. Mohrungen, founded at the beginning of the fourteenth century, grew around a castle of the Teutonic knights, in ruins during Herder's days. Herder's parents were poor but did not lack in the necessities of life. His father was a teacher, organist, and church warden, a taciturn and rigorously pious man who was a fanatic about punctuality and orderliness. His mother was as pious as her husband, yet more emotional and close to the child. The clergy of the time was of a moderate pietistic bent. Herder's two sisters remained in Mohrungen and were married to master craftsmen. A stern and pedantic, but fairly well-educated and dedicated schoolmaster named Grimm was in charge of the Latin school. Although Herder suffered from this harsh education, he became Grimm's favorite student. Beginning at the age of fourteen, he sometimes substituted for his father. He was a shy but studious boy who was interested in music and with a penchant for lonely walks. He stayed away from the usual exploits of small-town youngsters. At the age of sixteen he moved into the quarters of a vicar named Trescho, who wrote religious books and tracts and used Herder as his copyist in exchange for free lodging. Trescho had a good library, and Herder devoured volume after volume. However, he resented this arrangement, especially when Trescho counseled his parents against permitting him to attend university.

Liberation came through a Baltic surgeon named Schwartz-Erla who was stationed in Mohrungen with a Russian regiment and offered to take the young Herder with him to Königsberg to make him a surgeon. Herder fainted during the first operation he witnessed and used his last money to enroll as a student of theology. He was lucky to be accepted as a tutor at the Collegium Fridericianum, a pietistic boarding school with high standards, in exchange for free lodging. Soon he made money as a private tutor. He was then appointed teacher at the school, first for the lower, later also for the higher grades. In spite of his unconventional manners, like his refusal to wear a wig, he was respected and enjoyed phenomenal success as a teacher.

Even before coming to Königsberg, he had made his literary debut, smuggling an ode to Czar Peter III into a package from Trescho to a bookseller. He soon met Königsberg's literary figures and became friendly with Johann Georg Hamann (1730–87), the erratic and enigmatic writer and thinker, from whom he learned English by reading Shakespeare's plays. Hamann's ideas became crucial for Herder, and the two men remained close friends through correspondence, although their philosophical views differed in major aspects, which Herder usually glossed over in deference to his old friend. Herder also attended the lectures of the greatest mind at the University of Königsberg, Immanuel Kant. Kant was still years away from appointment to a professorship. As a private lecturer, he was forced to offer classes on a wide range of subjects in order to attract students. In fact, Herder, who attended Kant's lectures, enjoyed the classes on science and geography more than those on metaphysics.

Hamann's connections brought Herder an offer from the *Domschule* of Riga and he began his professional life there in 1764. Riga, an important seaport and trading center, was part of the Russian empire, but it had retained considerable autonomy. Although the capital of Latvia, it was dominated by the German middle class. Herder was easily accepted and became a successful teacher and preacher during the five years he stayed there. His first two books—*Über die neuere deutsche Literatur: Fragmente* (On recent German literature: fragments) and *Kritische Wälder* (Critical forests), published anonymously—brought with them notoriety, recognition, and finally fame. However, they also led to attacks that Herder could not handle well. Moreover, he began to feel restless, as he would do again and again in later life; on short notice, he left Riga in the summer of 1769 to go to France. He still planned to return to Riga, but he also considered a position as principal of the German school in St. Petersburg which had been offered to him. But his life took a different turn. After several months in Nantes, where he spent his time reading French literature and writing a "diary" of his voyage (a crucial document of his inner life, never to be published in his lifetime), he went on to Paris, his real destination; but this must have been anticlimatic. Little is known about his activities there:

his meeting with Diderot may have been the most important event. Herder disliked Paris, where he felt out of place. He was, therefore, happy to accept the offer of the prince-bishop of Oldenburg-Eutin to accompany his son on a three-year grand tour. Traveling through Holland, Herder experienced a dangerous shipwreck in the shallow coastal waters. He proceeded to Hamburg, where he spent two enjoyable weeks with Lessing and began his friendship with Matthias Claudius. He arrived in Eutin, where he encountered the pettiness and ridiculous hierarchy of a small court. The prince suffered from mental problems. He liked Herder, which caused frictions in the entourage, and increasingly the tour proved to be a disaster. Still, it gave him the opportunity to meet the two most important people in his life. In Darmstadt he became acquainted with Karoline Flachsland, an orphan living with her married sister. They fell in love immediately. Herder decided to quit his post. He went to Strassburg for an eye operation that would correct an old ailment and also make him more presentable. The procedure proved to be long, very painful, and costly, and only worsened his condition. In this uncomfortable state in the fall of 1770, uncertain about his future, he met a young law student named Goethe who was to describe this momentous meeting and its consequences in *Dichtung und Wahrheit*. Herder communicated to Goethe his ideas on folk songs, Shakespeare, Hebrew poetry in the Old Testament, the history of humankind, and language. Herder was then working on his *Abhandlung über den Ursprung der Sprache* (Treatise on the origin of language) that won the prize of the Prussian Academy of Sciences.

For lack of alternatives and in view of his marriage plans, Herder accepted the offer to be a court preacher and church official in the principality of Schaumburg-Lippe, with the capital of Bückeburg. Count Wilhelm of Schaumburg-Lippe had had a cordial relationship with the writer Thomas Abbt (1738–66), whose untimely death Herder had bemoaned in a sympathetic essay. But Herder was unlike Abbt, and when he arrived in Bückeburg in 1771, he received a cold welcome. Herder was too religious for the enlightened ruler and defended the rights of the church, even against the count himself. However, he was far too liberal for the provincial clergy and court society. He felt a little more content after his marriage in May 1773, but his official duties remained a heavy burden. He turned more intensively to writing and published the *Älteste Urkunde des Menschengeschlechts* (Oldest document of the human race) and *Noch eine Philosophie der Geschichte zur Bildung der Menschheit* (Another philosophy of history for the formation of humankind), both in 1774. He also wrote on theological topics and published a collection of short essays by himself, Goethe, and Justus Möser (1720–94) under the suggestive title of *Von deutscher Art und Kunst* (Of German kind and art), in 1773. He readied a collection of folk songs, but held back publication when he felt that his works, especially the *Oldest Document,* met with a hostile reception. He wanted to move to Göttingen as a professor of theology and university preacher, but his Lutheran colleagues made it so difficult that Herder was happy to accept the offer from Duke Karl August of Sachsen-Weimar, procured for him by Goethe, to come to Weimar as general super-intendent, constistorial councilor, and pastor of the court church.

Thus in 1776 Herder moved to Weimar, where he was to stay for the rest of his life, although he was never quite happy there. Herder liked to complain, but not without a reason. His plans for a reform of the church and the schools in the duchy of Sachsen-Weimar were hampered by lack of money. He was never able to enter into a close relationship with Karl August and influence gen-eral policy. In spite of his long and hard labors, he felt his efforts were largely wasted. Comparing himself to Martin Luther, he could not fail to see how little he achieved for an overall reform of society. He attributed these failures primarily to the narrow limits of the small states. Still, there was little choice. When the university of Göttingen belatedly made him an offer, in 1789, Herder, induced by some favorable financial arrangements, decided to stay in Weimar.

After an initial warm welcome by Goethe, the two men found it difficult to adjust to the new constellation in their relationship. Goethe was no longer the immature Strassburg student, while Her-der was not the superior leader and teacher. They were equals, and Herder hated to ask Goethe, the duke's minister, for favors. Goethe's elevation to nobility and promotion in the administration cut short a brief phase of understanding. Finally, the celebration of Goethe's birthday in August 1783 broke the ice and ushered in a period of mutual friendship and close collaboration. This friendship was clouded, however, by political differences after the French Revo-lution, and in 1793–95 disagreements concerning the duke's prom-ises aggravated the situation. The duke had promised to provide for the education of Herder's many sons, but the question was how. In the ensuing conflict, Goethe tried to mediate, only to be rebuked by the Herders, Karoline in particular. A compromise was finally found, but the trusting relationship between Herder and Goethe was never restored, despite several attempts by Goethe. Goethe's celebrated alliance with Schiller, beginning in June 1794, helped to worsen the situation, since Herder disliked Schiller. He found himself, as it were, replaced by Schiller as Goethe's first critic and advisor in his literary production. Herder was certainly capable of being jealous.

Again, the conflict went deeper. The impact of Herder's conception of life and literature on Goethe was deep and lasting, yet the two men differed on several accounts. Goethe ceased to believe in Herder's view of the public function of literature and the idea of a nation state. These disagreements came to the fore after 1789. Herder wrote some of his most important works at the time of his friendship with Goethe, but his later productions should be given more credit, even if Goethe disapproved of them.

Herder kept developing the essay form and submitted quite a few essays for competitions sponsored by various German academies. Although he received a number of prizes, some of the most significant essays were rejected, notably *Über das Erkennen und Empfinden der menschlichen Seele* (On the cognition and sensation of the human soul, 1778). In Weimar, Herder first completed and published some earlier projects, especially a collection of folk songs, generally known by a title that was not Herder's own, *Stimmen der Völker in Liedern* (Voices of the peoples in songs). Herder published his *Plastik* (Plastic Arts) and *Vom Geist der Ebräischen Poesie* (On the spirit of Hebrew poetry). But most importantly, the need for a new edition of *Another philosophy* resulted in Herder's central work, *Ideen zur Philosophie der Geschichte der Menschheit* (Ideas on the philosophy of the history of humankind), published in four parts between 1784 and 1791. He also published *Briefe das Studium der Theologie betreffend* (Letters concerning the study of theology) and, in 1787, his Platonic dialogue on the Spinoza controversy, entitled *Gott*.

Herder's journey to Italy in 1788–89 was undertaken initially to accompany, for financial reasons, a man named von Dalberg. However, when Dalberg's mistress unexpectedly came along as well, things became unpleasant, and Herder and Dalberg separated in Rome. In spite of pleasant moments, especially in Naples, Herder did not find the rejuvenation in Italy that Goethe had found there.

Herder's *Ideas* are generally considered the high point of his writing career. The outbreak of the French Revolution, however, made the completion of the work difficult. Herder never wrote the fifth, concluding part that would have treated the recent past. Instead, he began a collection of *Briefe zu Beförderung der Humanität* (Letters for the advancement of humanity). The original plan to offer a commentary on contemporary events could not be carried out for reasons of censorship and because of the rapidly changing situation. The *Letters* content themselves with rather indirect statements. In view of Duke Karl August's and Goethe's participation in the interventionist wars of 1792 and 1793 against France, Herder had a hard time maintaining his faith in progress and his advocacy of a republican form of government.

It was out of disgust with the impact of politics on personal lives that Goethe liked Schiller's project of a nonpolitical journal, *Die Horen*. Herder became part of the original planning group for the journal and contributed several essays and poems, but he soon disliked the fact that the journal did not reflect a position above politics, but rather against the changes initiated by the revolution. A journal in a liberal humanistic spirit, as was planned, may have been impossible to achieve. Herder still championed a truly popular national literature for the general public, and not what he considered elitist art works for an esoteric circle. This conflict caused a bitter altercation between Herder and Schiller and led to Herder's ultimate withdrawal. Herder was also increasingly hostile to the vogue of Kantianism, as personified by Schiller and Johann Gottlieb Fichte (1762–1814), then a professor of philosophy in Jena.

Kant and Herder remained on friendly terms, although not close, until Kant wrote harsh reviews on the first two parts of the *Ideas*. Herder, like Hamann, strongly objected to Kant's *Critique of Pure Reason,* but it took him many years before he spoke out in his *Metakritik zur Kritik der reinen Vernunft* (Metacritique of the *Critique of Pure Reason,* 1799), to be followed by *Kalligone,* a critique of Kant's aesthetics. Indirectly, Herder also aimed at Schiller's aesthetic writings.

Herder grew increasingly disenchanted with his own age. Still, with the exception of his attacks on Kantian philosophy, he refrained from open polemics. His late works are mostly collections of shorter essays, translations, and his own poetic creations. This is typical for *Zerstreute Blätter* (Scattered leaves), for the *Letters for the Advancement of Humanity,* and the last collection, *Adrastea,* which remained unfinished. In it, Herder tried to summarize the significant trends of eighteenth-century history and culture. He also summarized his religious beliefs in his so-called "Christian writings," mostly studies on the New Testament. Containing many interesting features, these writings are distinguished by one basic contradiction: a perspicacious liberal view of the history of mankind as a whole combined with a harsh indictment of his own age.

Herder stayed in Weimar, overburdened by administrative duties, tirelessly fighting for better churches and schools, and feeling frustrated by the smallness of the duchy, by personal animosities, and the restrictions of censorship of all kinds. He was happy in his family and saw his children grow up as good human beings. In spite of some improvements, the Herder family never grew out of financial worries and constant debts. In the last years of his life, Herder was rather isolated. The communication with Schiller and Goethe was cut off, and the Jena circle of romantics kept a respectful distance from him. Only the friendship of Jean Paul Richter, who came to Weimar on a visit in 1796 and lived there from 1798 to 1800, mitigated this isolation. More and more frequent illnesses interrupted Herder's work, and he went to different spas to restore his health. Constantly working, he succumbed to his many ailments on 18 December 1803 and was buried with all the honors due to the highest church official of the duchy of Sachsen-Weimar; but the literary world had little to say, with the exception of the moving epilogue in Jean Paul's *School of Aesthetics* (1804). Karoline, who died in 1809, organized the first collection of Herder's works and brought together materials for a volume of documents and recollections.

Herder's impact on his age and on the nineteenth century was great, but it often went unacknowledged, and a double image prevailed: that of the stimulator of the generation of the *Sturm und Drang,* especially Goethe, and that of the hostile critic of Kantian philosophy and German *Klassik.* It is time to go beyond these contradictions and present a more differentiated view of his life and work.

Chapter Two
A Restless Young Mind
A Young Poet and Preacher

Herder's first published work was an ode to Czar Peter III. Throughout his life, Herder wrote poetry, most of which he did not publish. As a young man, however, he had high hopes and ambitions. His great model was Klopstock; but Herder was also preoccupied with didactic poetry. As a student in Königsberg, he transformed one of Kant's lectures into a poem that pleased Kant so much that he read it aloud to his class. Although Herder championed the cause of the revival of the folk song and admired Goethe's poetry, his own poetic style was closer to the generation of Klopstock.

There was one major reason for this affinity. Herder saw poetry as a public means of communication and not as a medium for the expression of private feelings. He did not publish poems that he considered too intimate. Poetry was therefore a variation of public speaking. Herder did not subscribe to the emerging separation of the poetic and rhetorical genres. His poems deal with the general themes of the period: God, immortality, fatherland, friendship, love, human nature, just ruler and good government, and conviviality. They are audience directed, just like Schiller's or Hölderlin's. Herder's writings were never an end in themselves but substitutes for social action, or a preparation of such action. As he himself expressed it in his *Journal,* his dream was to become a reformer of society, a second Martin Luther. While he lived among books and wrote books, he wanted to break out of the book world into the real world of social action and decision making. All of his writings were designed to have an impact on their readers, and that is, according to rhetorical tradition, both an intellectual and an emotional impact. The wide range of Herder's writings is in inverse proportion to the small range of social activities that were permitted to him. He was largely a writer because of lack of opportunity for other activities.

In Riga, Herder found opportunities for speeches and sermons that were well received, and for journal articles. These topical pieces, however, forecast Herder's central preoccupations. *Über den Fleiss in mehreren gelehrten Sprachen* (On the diligence in several learned languages) is a short essay published in 1764, but presumably based on a speech dating from the Königsberg days.[1] Ostensibly it deals with the relative importance of instruction in the mother tongue and in foreign languages, a topic dear to Herder, who objected to the overemphasis on Latin in the school curriculum. But the essay goes much beyond this primary purpose. Rhetorically, it moves from rational and utilitarian arguments to higher ranges and wider perspectives, and ends with a quotation of poetry. In a few pages, Herder offers a sketch of the history of human civilization. There was an original unity in language and culture. When peoples and languages separated, their languages began to express the character of their specific civilizations, determined by history and geography. Thus each language has become the expression of innermost cultural experiences, and in turn determines the *Denkart,* the way of thinking of people. Attention to an understanding and proper use of one's own language is therefore mandatory. No people, however, could be culturally self-sufficient, nor would that be beneficial for the culture. Cross-cultural relations, synchronic and diachronic, are needed. And it is only through the medium of the foreign language that other cultures can be experienced. Therefore, the need for learning foreign languages is vital; and they should be learned like one's own language, if possible. Only in that manner could one absorb the spirit of that language and the essence of the culture, and go beyond meaningless grammatical structures. However, a scholar who immerses himself in the past age of a foreign culture without being at home in his own culture, cuts a ridiculous figure.

Language and thought are indivisible. Language is a key to thinking, learning, and life. Languages have a history; they change with the climate, the environment, and the historical conditions. The biblical story of the Tower of Babel opens the perspective of the idea of one human language versus the idea of many languages. The present fragmented condition of a multitude of languages makes the need for cross-cultural communication even greater. Since translation is transfer from one culture to another, communication cannot be achieved through translation, but only through familiarity with the other languages. Only in such a manner could diversity be overcome and a new unity of mankind approached. Such a future unity would therefore be based upon a diversity of national languages. However, only the proper awareness of one's own language and culture provides the key to other cultures. The mother tongue is largely subconscious and part of our childhood impressions. No other language can be learned in the same way; still, comparisons and wider perspectives are essential for a better future.

Herder was pondering the practical consequences of this view, as can be seen from his *Journal*. He wanted languages to be taught as, and together with, *realia*. They should not be separated from geography and history, and not reduced to excercises in abstract logic. The learning of one's own language and that of foreign languages should complement one another, always considering the learning of the mother tongue the primary responsibility.

From his pedagogical preoccupations, Herder thus developed a nucleus of a language theory, and a perspective on the development of human cultures. His essay should be seen together with the speech, *Haben wir noch jetzt das Publikum und Vaterland der Alten?* (Do we still have the public and fatherland of the ancients?). The address was given in 1765, in connection with the opening of a new court house in Riga. It gains added significance by the fact that Herder reworked it late in life for the *Letters for the Advancement of Humanity*.[2] The primary issue is public speaking. It was common in eighteenth-century Germany to deplore the decline in public speaking skills. Herder went beyond technical considerations to point out essential cultural reasons. Athens could have a public forum because it had an undifferentiated society: every citizen was prepared to lead the army, make laws, and administer the city. Modern society demands more specialized knowledge and skills. But a society based entirely on specialization and self-interest—as envisioned in the books of Claude Adrien Helvetius (1715–71)—could not have any of the patriotic spirit demanded by Thomas Abbt in his book *On the Death for One's Fatherland* (1761). Herder was speaking to the upper class of a self-governing city-state. He had reasons to emphasize *bürgerliche Freiheit*, freedom in one's own sphere of activity, and a liberal relationship between church and state. Beyond working for one's own legitimate self-interest, a communal spirit is needed. The speech ends with an ode to the city of Riga praising freedom, justice, God, and patriotism.

At that time Herder could not foresee the dangers of chauvinism. He was keenly aware of the dangers of absolutism, such as court intrigues, corruption, flattery, influence buying, and selfishness of the higher classes, while the people remained passive victims of exploitation. How to overcome such conditions? The communal spirit of the ancients could not be duplicated under such different historical conditions. A new type of communal spirit was needed. Public speaking had to be an essential ingredient for such spirit. Herder was also speaking *pro domo,* since the churches were among the few public places where public speeches were possible. But, what of the separation of religious and civil matters? Herder's picture is optimistic and harmonizing, as is fitting for a festive occasion. He leaves a number of questions unanswered and is careful not to go too far in his criticism. His basic theme is clear: without a communal spirit, articulated by poets and speakers, a country cannot thrive. There cannot be a nation, much less a great nation, without an eloquent and deep-reaching expression of the national spirit. Culture and society are interdependent. Real impact is achieved by popular culture; true poetry communicates the essential emotions, whereas intellectual precision, sophistication, and artificiality will never change society. Herder's speeches, sermons, and poems aimed at "that venerable part of the nation, the people,"[3] and thus he tried to be direct and simple, without talking down to anybody. In his draft of a sermon, "God's Rhetor" (Oer Redner Gottes)[4] Herder emphasized that the preacher should take his concrete evidence from his listeners' own experience, and that he should view their daily lives "in the light of reflection." Herder the preacher always remained mindful of his audience. He never hesitated to address basic concerns, and in Weimar he confronted the duke—on the rare occasions that he attended church—with sermons on the duties of a ruler.[5]

Herder's first writings are a nucleus of his ambitions and thoughts. They are far-reaching yet practical, and motivated by immediate political and pedagogical concerns. They are optimistic, as they reflect the hopes of a young man of letters who is recognized by his society, and who can hope to influence the course of events. Herder saw that the major drawback was the lack of an outlet for the expression of the voice of the people such as enjoyed by the people of Israel, the citizens of Athens, and the inhabitants of Shakespeare's England. This critical attitude toward his own age was still tempered by the hope that reform may be possible. Public-spirited poetry and the free expression of public issues could and should have a major impact on the direction of society and the building of nations. There is a clear implication that such a new communal spirit might not be generated by the enlightened middle class, but would have to come from the common people, but Herder still refused to accept antagonisms of this kind. Whereas his views were liberal, he did not see progress in the direction of progressive secularization, but in a renewal of religion and its integration into modern life. During this period, "Human philosophy," or *Humanität,* as he was to call it later,[6] emerged as the center of his preoccupations. The human condition, determined by language, and thus by historical traditions and geographical conditions, aspires at an overcoming of separations, social, cultural, and national. Cosmopolitism, however, is not reached through a disregard of ethnic entities, but only through a firm grounding in one's own culture. From this basis arises the respect for other cultures. The human being is complete only in its own natural environment. Human philosophy in Herder's way would be interested in the entire human being, not in separate faculties. *Ganzheit,* completeness, is the precondition for the study of mankind, past and present.

Calling for a National Literature

In Riga, Herder was a member of the socially dominant cultural minority. From his vantage point outside of the German-language area, he saw German literature as a whole, and thus he brought one of his many projects—an assessment of current German literature— to a partial conclusion. The daring of the young man in his early twenties to undertake this task can only be compared to the audacious manner with which Jean Jacques Rousseau burst on the French scene. Herder's professor Kant was an ardent admirer of Rousseau, especially of *Émile* (1762), and Herder was certainly mindful of the success of this poor man from the people, from the outskirts of French culture.

Herder's method was peculiar and looks at first sight derivative. He took the most representative literary journal of his time and wrote something like a review on reviews, a commentary on commentaries. The *Briefe, die neueste Literatur betreffend* had been the brainchild of Lessing and were published by the enterprising Friedrich Nicolai. After Lessing entered the Prussian military administration in 1760, the journal was carried on by Moses Mendelssohn and Nicolai, later joined by Thomas Abbt and other occasional contributors. In 1765, the journal had run its course, and Nicolai replaced it with his monumental *Allgemeine Deutsche Bibliothek,* which, in the spirit of the Enlightenment, reviewed books in all fields of knowledge.

Herder wrote, as it were, a commentary on the entire *Letters*—twenty-four volumes including index. He did not complete his original plan—a fate typical of most of Herder's works. He planned to move from language to belles lettres, history, and finally philosophy, but never arrived at the last two sections, thus creating the false impression that he spoke solely as a literary critic. He reviewed literature in its broadest meaning, prose and poetry writing on any subject, certainly including history and religion.

Herder's *Über die neuere deutsche Literatur: Fragmente* focuses first on language. Most significant is the section "Über die verschiedenen Lebensalter einer Sprache," on the different life stages of a language: "Just as the human being appears in different life stages, time changes everything. The entire human race, the inanimate world itself, each nation, and each family are subject to the same law of change: from bad to good, from good to excellent, from excellent to worse, and to bad: this is the circular movement of all things. Thus it is for every art and science: they germinate, have buds, blossom, and fade away. The same is true for language" (SW, 1:151–52). Herder attacks the idea of linear progress. History is development, evolution; but that should not be seen as the perfection of a machine. Rather, history has to be compared to the life stages of plants. Every stage reaches its own perfection but must give way to the next. Human culture, Herder argues, should be interpreted through organicistic models rather than through mechanistic ones.[7] The human body is not like a clock, and history does not move solely from bad to good. On the contrary, it moves in cycles. With these views, Herder was in step with the biological sciences of his time,[8] but he opposed many of the inferences that Enlightenment thinkers had drawn from modern physics and mathematics for the social sciences, including history and psychology.

The application of such a view to language communication is evident. Language is not an arbitrary convention among people, nor is it "made" like a machine. Therefore, it cannot be changed at will, but it develops according to the life stages of human culture. If Herder's German contemporaries called for an improvement of the German language in order to create a national literature, they

were mostly overlooking these fundamental points. In any historical
change, there is both gain and loss, a fact overlooked by the believers
in linear progress. Specifically, it is the language of primitive cultures that is truly poetic. "Poetry is the mother tongue of humanity,"
had been Hamann's defiant statement, which Herder was to repeat
and amplify for the rest of his life. The growing refinement of
culture causes poetry to be changed into prose; intellectual accuracy
replaces musical harmony and beauty of the language. At the end
of the cycle, which began with poetic primitivism, stands the philosophical age of learned prose. It is easy to recognize the eighteenth
century in Herder's description of the philosophical age. If the real
value of language lies in its untranslatable idioms rather than in
intellectual formulations common to various civilizations, the ex-
treme intellectualization of a language cannot be considered a gain.

Herder urged his readers to follow the contemporary masters of
German poetry and prose to improve their style. He mentioned
Winckelmann, the poet Hagedorn, the political writer and states-
man Friedrich Karl Moser (1723–98), the theologian Johann Joachim
Spalding (1714–1804), Thomas Abbt, Moses Mendelssohn, Les-
sing, Justus Möser, Klopstock, and, last but not least, Hamann.

In the second collection of the *Fragments,* Herder applies his
concept of language and culture to literary criticism. The critic, he
says, should be a friend of the author, entering into the spirit and
intentions of the work and judging it from its own premises. Herder
emphatically rejects ahistorical, absolute standards and predeter-
mined sets of criteria. Certainly the danger inherent in this intuitive
and historical procedure is a lack of inner distance from the object;
however, this procedure accurately detects whether the author pre-
serves the spirit of his language and culture.

With all this emphasis on originality, enhanced by references to
Edward Young's *Conjectures on Original Composition* (*SW,* 1:256), it
seems surprising that Herder deals with imitation and influence.
But he had to combat the tradition that compared contemporary
writers with the great models and would routinely designate certain
German poets "the German Pindar" or "the German Homer." What
does this mean, and in which sense could it be justified? Creative
reception is not an imitation of a great model. A genius, Herder
maintains, does not create *ex nihilo;* he needs examples and can only
be stimulated by another genius. But it is the characteristic trait

of a genius to transform such models into the spirit and language of his own time and to observe essentials rather than formal details.

Thus Herder asks whether Oriental, Greek, Latin, and other literatures can be imitated, or rather transformed into German originals, and how successful such attempts by contemporary writers have been. Hebrew poetry, like the songs and the psalms of the Bible, are the expression of the national spirit, of an ancient people of the Middle East. It is anything but easy to transfer images natural for a Jew or Arab into Central European conditions. The *Geist der Religion,* spirit of religion (*SW,* 1:267), has changed as well. How can a national religion be expressed at a time of universal religions? A translator has to be a philologist, a poet, and a philosopher at the same time (*SW,* 1:274). Herder dismisses mediocre products in passing, but discusses Klopstock's *Messias* at length. Since the work was then far from completed, he offers constructive criticism. He gives hints for the completion of the work. This is not done dogmatically, but by means of a dialogue between a Jewish rabbi and a Christian. The rabbi criticizes the lack of specifically Jewish traits, whereas the Christian wants Klopstock to avoid wrong imitations of predecessors such as Vergil and Milton. The dialogue partners both insist on concrete action and description. They warn Klopstock against too much abstraction. Indeed they have high expectations for the outstanding parts of the work.

Herder dwells at length on the virtues of antique Greek poetry and on the need as well as the difficulties of adequate translations into German. In fact, he wants translations with notes in order to come closer to the original. While he warns against imitations of Homer, he considers German Anacreontic poetry close to the original, and he lauds the efforts by Willamovius to imitate Pindar's dithyrambic style. Willamovius remained an obscure East Prussian poet, but Herder's prediction came true: Pindar became a powerful inspiration for German poets like Goethe, Hölderlin, and Nietzsche.

Herder's third collection discusses the impact of the Latin language and Latin poetry on Germany. While he argues persuasively against a slavish imitation of the Latin style, he differentiates carefully between useful and harmful influences. The dominant role of the Latin language is a fact; and while it is of prime importance to revive the German national spirit, this cannot be done by simply rejecting Latin. Still, the first duty of German schools is to teach the mother tongue and to develop a sensitivity for the values of language through one's native language.

Herder by no means rejects Latin literature. He praises the poet Ramler for his Horatian odes, he deals with elegies, and he is especially interested in the Lucretian didactic poem, to which he ascribes high value. Herder thought at the time that he could revive the didactic poem as a synthesis of poetry and philosophy, suitable for his "philosophical" age.[9] Of considerable historical importance is Herder's little essay in this collection "Vom neueren Gebrauch der Mythologie," which signals the end of a purely decorative and allegorical use of mythological figures and events in literature and the arts. A new awareness of the significance of mythology was emerging and articulated itself against the traditional erudition, which was so absorbed by details that it lost the sense for the significance of mythology as such.

Herder's *Fragments* do not signal a break with the Enlightenment. He honored the best German writers, irrespective of their labeling by later historians. He saw German literature as a whole, not in factions. It is a pity that he did not complete the sections on imitations of French and English literature, because it is more than likely that, contrary to the expectations of most scholars, he would not have come off as a Francophobe and Anglomaniac. Herder's arguments were more stimulating than well-rounded, but he called for a national consciousness rather than a partisan spirit. He wanted a renewal of the poetic spirit for the German nation. This new spirit, while it might be stimulated by the Psalms, Pindar, Shakespeare, and folk songs, would have to have a uniquely German character.

It may be that Herder envisioned the impossible: the spirit of early poetry integrated into a philosophical age. But his call for a poetic renewal was timely, and in this sense one may say that at an early stage of his career he became the *praeceptor Germaniae*.

For a New Approach in Aesthetics

In 1769 Herder published *Kritische Wälder, Oder Betrachtungen die Wissenschaft und Kunst des Schönen betreffend, nach Maasgabe neuerer Schriften* (Critical Forests, Or reflections concerning the science and art of the beautiful, measured by recent writings). Three "Groves" appeared; the fourth, partially completed, remained unpublished in Herder's lifetime. The work, like the *Fragments,* appeared anonymously. Even the name of the publisher and the place of publication were missing. Such practice was not uncommon in an age of censorship, but Herder was foolish when he believed he could hide his identity. Gossip, curiosity, and a keen sense of stylistic features identified anonymous writers in a short time. Against the advice of Hamann and Friedrich Nicolai, who had liked and praised the *Fragments,* Herder persisted in denying his authorship of the *Critical Forests.* They were controversial, and he felt uneasy as a teacher and clergyman for having produced them. His public denials worsened the situation. The affair was soon forgotten, of course, but Herder felt his social position in Riga had been damaged, and imagined a loss of reputation in the literary world. The controversy proved to be his ultimate motivation for leaving Riga.

The whole episode of the publication of the *Critical Forests* may not be significant, but it reveals Herder's basic dilemma as a writer. He was at times a severe critic of his age and of contemporary literature, but he was not ready to accept the ensuing attacks on himself. He had a thin skin and was not prepared to fight his battles as a free-lance writer and free spirit, an emerging species at the time.[10] In contrast to Lessing, or even Hamann, Herder could never see himself as just a writer. While he relished and demanded the freedom of social criticism, he considered himself part of governmental authority. The public-spirited official as writer was common in the German Enlightenment, but in Herder's case, not unlike Goethe's, contradictions became apparent and separation of government and public opinion became inevitable.

Questions of aesthetic theory may be an unlikely ground for such conflicts. However, the public relevance of aesthetic thinking was considerable. The assertion of new principles against the classical and French tradition and the justification for the establishment of middle-class art against court entertainment had broad political implications. Lessing had attacked the established mediocrities of his day not only to set new standards, but also to pave the way for works with a new message.

Lessing's *Laokoon*—which was to become one of the central texts in the discussion of aesthetics—had just appeared. Herder's first "Grove" provided an important critique of this work. The other two "Groves" are polemical and deal with inferior and now forgotten adversaries. The first "Grove" starts out as a running commentary on Lessing's treatise. Herder objects, modifies, and criticizes, while stressing the significance of Lessing's arguments. Lessing had argued against Winckelmann, and Herder defends Winckelmann against Lessing. They are both partially right, Lessing as a literary critic, Winckelmann as an art critic. However, Herder disagreed with Lessing's interpretations of Greek literature as well. He considered Lessing's distinctions between literature and the pictorial arts too unspecified. There was much more decorum in Greek drama and epic poetry than Lessing admitted, and literature should be judged in terms of the historical conditions and the conventions of the literary genres in mind. The same arguments prevail in Herder's critique of Lessing's interpretations of Latin poetry, notably Vergil.

Furthermore, while Lessing had talked about the visual arts in general, Herder insisted on fundamental differences between painting and sculpture. Arguing with James Harris's *Three Treatises* (1744), he distinguishes forms of art that constitute a "work," such as painting and sculpture, from those whose effect is successive and thus "energy," like music and dance. On the other hand, painting, music, and poetry are mimetic—they imitate through different media. They imitate bodies and colors (painting), movements and sounds (music), or both (poetry). Herder makes a much more differentiated usage of Lessing's principles of succession and simultaneity. He is also beginning to insist on the connection between the human senses and the various art forms. He discusses the place of ugliness in art and its relationship to the comic, and makes it clear that he is not bound by a classicist canon.

Scholars differ on the relative merits of Lessing's and Herder's arguments.[11] Lessing was inspired and encouraged by Herder's critique, but unfortunately, he did not complete the second part of *Laokoon*.[12] Lessing had demonstrated the generic absurdity of purely descriptive poetry. Herder fine-tuned Lessing's analyses. Most of all, he insisted on the sensual and expressive qualities of the arts. He attacked artificial art that did not express the true spirit of its age and culture and did not reveal the depth of human nature.

In the second and third "Groves," Herder fought against representatives of the past. Christian Adolf Klotz (1738–71) was a professor of classics at the University of Halle who had gained a reputation for elegant Latin style and supposed erudition. He had an enormous command of details, but no real penetration of the Greek and Latin spirit. With vanity, even arrogance, he wielded power through his journals, *Acta Litteraria* and *Bibliothek der Schönen Wissenschaften,* as well as through his writings and those of his students and followers. Klotz had opened the attack, stung by a very mild criticism in the *Fragments* (*SW*, 1:426–29).

As it happened, Herder's "Groves" appeared shortly after Lessing's *Antiquarian Letters* (1768–69) had demolished Klotz. This was a typical literary feud, but it was more than a victory of excellence over mediocrity. Lessing and Herder were not *Gelehrte* (erudites) in the old sense. They wrote about Homer and Pindar because these poets were relevant for the present age and society. They were not interested in philology for its own sake but wanted to understand the past and bring it back to life. The study of facts was replaced by historical empathy.

Herder's two "Groves" are too long to be entertaining. He first dissects Klotz's letters on Homer, then Klotz's reading of Vergil. In both cases, he presents a new concept of the epic genre. The reason that Klotz found "faults" in Homer, Herder argues, was that he did not understand him. Herder's arguments are particularly strong when he comments on Homer's use of comic scenes and characters within the framework of the elevated style. Klotz's conventional classicism could not grasp the function of such scenes.

The third "Grove" deals with cut stones, their symbols and inscriptions, a current topic, but hardly an attractive issue for the twentieth century. With some regret, Herder sighed at the end: "Yet, how much time have I lost—" (*SW*, 3:480).

The second and third "Groves" are unique in Herder's career, and he did not feel good about them in spite of their success. Lessing's *Antiquarian Letters* were much sharper, wittier, and more concise. Herder did not know how to deal with an insignificant adversary. He never tried it again. His subsequent polemics were to have worthy objects.

The uneasy feeling may have been the main reason why he did not complete the promising fourth "Grove," which began as an attack on one of Klotz's favorite students, Friedrich Justus Riedel (1742–86), professor at the University of Erfurt. In 1767 Riedel had published a *Theorie der schönen Künste und Wissenschaften* (Theory of the arts and aesthetics), which was intended to popularize the new science of aesthetics. Herder went far beyond demonstrating the shallowness and mindless eclecticism of this "theory." He wanted to lay his own foundation for the study of the arts. He developed his earlier idea that the different forms of art were related to sense perceptions. While most terms of aesthetic theory derived from the visual field, and the importance of hearing could not be denied, Herder insisted on the significance of *Gefühl* (touch). This alone could provide the idea of bodily nature, and thus provide the foundation for sculpture and the plastic arts in general. Touch brings closeness, whereas the visual sense is one of distance. The sense of touch is more elementary, basic, and primitive than the others. At the same time, Herder insists on unity: "How beautiful the human soul becomes in this manner! Fundamental unity, variety, a thousand times multiplied, in its development, perfection in the sum of the whole!" (*SW,* 4:34). Our potential sense for the beautiful, from which everything springs, needs to be developed to allow for taste and understanding. This is like a seed containing the potential for the full organism. In general, the human being enters this world with a potential whose realization depends on cultural and historical conditions, not with ready-made faculties.

The fourth "Grove" was not published in a reliable version until 1878. This is a pity, although some of its ideas were used in later published works. Still Herder had introduced himself to the German world of letters as a formidable critic and writer on aesthetics, and as a fresh voice, expressing new and untried ideas.

A So-Called Travel Diary

When Herder stayed in Nantes preparing himself for the visit to Paris, he felt that he had to take stock of his life and map out his future. He tried to communicate with himself in the form of a "travel diary" which he called *Journal meiner Reise im Jahr 1769* (Diary of my voyage in 1769). This is a misnomer, since the journal was written after the fact. It is not a record of actual experiences, but a sequence of reflections, expression of feelings, and description of projects with little apparent order. It may have been intended for publication, for Herder's financial situation was disastrous, but it turned out to be a very private document, and Herder chose to keep it for himself. Scholars have hailed it as the beginning of the Storm and Stress movement and as the introduction of a new sensibility into German letters. But this remained hidden from contemporaries. Herder was twenty-five years old, and he had a unique opportunity to look at himself and the world around him.

A basic contradiction in the *Diary* remains unresolved. Herder chides himself for too much reading, too much book learning, too much writing. He has never touched reality and squandered his life to live in a world of books. And yet, he sketches plans for books that would take more than a lifetime to complete, and that would condemn the author to more reading and writing. He is torn between his hunger for direct involvement and his need to complete the great document of his ideas.

A good part of the *Diary* is taken up with very concrete plans. Herder was still thinking about the German school in St. Petersburg or about being principal of the *Gymnasium* in Riga. Therefore he planned school curricula. Beyond the emphasis on German and the down-grading of Latin grammar, he stressed the teaching of reality and reminded himself to relate the teaching material to the experience of the students. Above all, he insisted on the unity of all learning. All disciplines are interconnected and should be taught as such. The students should be educated for their future positions in society. Precisely because they would be specialists, a universalist outlook was needed. This alone would ensure that each profession would consider itself part of a whole, of a mutually interdependent organism.

Herder's ambitions went beyond the education of the future elite. He saw himself as a reformer of *Kurland*, the Baltic countries, or even Russia as a whole. He wanted to set the stage for a new age of liberty and humanity. That alone would give meaning to his life: "I am going through the world; what do I have in it, if I do not make myself immortal?" (*SW* 4:401). His writing is meant to be a preparation for action. Therefore, he has to get closer to life itself.

The central project he plots is an *Universalgeschichte der Bildung der Welt* (*SW,* 4:353), a universal history of the formation of the world—*Bildung* (formation) denoting all processes of creation, development, and education. Compared to this project, the *Ideas* seem to be of modest proportions. This should not be a book for scholars, Herder muses, but a book that changes the world, a book like those of Rousseau, of Montesquieu, the lawgiver, of Martin Luther, the reformer. He could be, he hopes, a second Montesquieu, a new Luther for the Baltic States, for Russia.

Herder's overview of the cultures of Europe in his *Diary* seems to be an examination for where he might want to live and work. He examines the world as he examines himself. It is a "work in progress." He tests new ideas, challenges them, overrules objections, and reformulates them. The *Diary* is a grandiose monologue with different voices. In the face of far-reaching, even utopian dreams, he has to tell himself that certain things might not be feasible.

Much has been made of Herder's critique of French literature. He had high hopes for his visit to France. He had wanted to perfect himself in language, manners, and education. But he saw French culture in its decline. There was much less to learn than he had thought. His perspective, moreover, was influenced by social critics like Montesquieu, Voltaire, and Rousseau. Herder was not "anti-French," but he decided that French culture was not a model to follow. He learned a great deal from French authors, Rousseau above all, but his stay in France convinced him that other cultures needed their own approaches. Even more importantly, French culture was still centered around the court and a small group of intellectuals. The renewal of culture that Herder advocated had to come from below, from the people. The Prussian King Frederick II was wrong when he thought he could transplant Paris to Berlin.

The *Diary* is a grandiose, but also a disturbing document. Herder thinks and dreams in ever wider circles, and associates idea with idea, metaphor with metaphor, until he reaches a point of vast vision, an infinite horizon, as it were. Then he catches himself, makes a new start, and goes off into a different direction.[13] The *Diary* is punctuated by Herder's favorite stylistic devices: dashes, exclamation marks, underlined words, rhetorical questions. His mind is working, but also drifting. He stands between daring enterprise and pietistic introspection, unable to decide which way to go. There is an incongruity between inner vision and outer reality, between his potential and the real possibilities for social action. Even more, Herder is torn between contemplation and action, expansion and withdrawal.

The social model that could make his dreams come true is that of the philosopher king, the wise ruler who could be guided by a farsighted councilor. Ever since his Riga experience Herder kept advocating a "republic," but the concept of "republic," especially that of Plato, did not contradict the notion of a philosopher king. In the context of eighteenth-century Germany and Russia, such a king would be needed to help educate the people. Only after a process of education, the population would be able to make intelligent choices. Thus a wise ruler would indeed be needed to bring about a society of responsible and community-minded individuals.

Herder never completed the *Diary*. In its literary form, it shows traces of the pietistic autobiography, travel literature, and political memoirs. No genre really fits. The ocean and the ship remain central images. Herder never forgot the contrast between the infinite sea and the narrow ship with its strict social structure. While the visit to France failed to give him the desired exposure to social life, he had experienced the elements of nature on the voyage and acquired a deeper understanding of primitive man, mythology, and natural phenomena. It reinforced Herder's sensualism, his reliance on sense-related data rather than on philosophical systems. A metaphor or a mythological image may contain more reality than abstract concepts.

The *Diary* is not a break with the Enlightenment. Herder does not abandon reason, but he insists on the integration of all faculties and sees mankind within the natural environment and as part of it. Although humanity is fundamentally different from animality, humans have many things in common with other living beings. The *Diary* is anything but a systematic philosophy. It is the largely spontaneous expression of ruminations, feelings, and ideas. It is a highly revealing private document indicating Herder's position between different cultures and different periods.

The Origin of Language

When Goethe met Herder in Strassburg in the fall of 1770, he was surprised to learn that the latter was writing a treatise on a strange topic. Herder was competing for the prize of the Prussian Academy of Sciences on the question of the origin of language. Specifically, the academy was asking whether human language was of divine or human origin. Johann Peter Süssmilch (1706–67) had brought new attention to this age-old question with his 1766 treatise that tried to prove that the creator, not man himself, was the maker of the first language. Süssmilch's treatise has interesting aspects[14], and the academy, a champion of Enlightenment, felt challenged, especially since the philosophy of language was a favorite topic among its members.[15] Herder wrote in great haste to meet the deadline, but he was ready for the challenge. He received the prize, to his real surprise and satisfaction, and this initial success encouraged him to write other prize essays, quite a few of which received prizes. This tenacity is somewhat puzzling, although the prize money was always welcome. Herder had an ambiguous attitude toward the institutions and most of the questions posed by them. Sometimes, he seems not to answer the question, but to demonstrate its absurdity. Still, Herder hoped that the academies might develop into institutions for the free exchange of views on relevant public issues.

Some scholars have also detected an ironic tone in Herder's *Abhandlung über den Ursprung der Sprache* (Treatise on the origin of language). Herder gave a complex answer that could be interpreted in different ways. It obviously pleased the academy but greatly perturbed Hamann, who was convinced of the divine origin of language.

Herder argued on two fronts. He rejected Süssmilch's theory of a divine origin of human language, but he also denied that humans acquired language naturally, like animals, as Condillac and Rousseau seemed to have said. There is animal language, Herder agrees, and the human being participates in it. This language consists in emotional responses to certain situations, expressed in simple sounds. This layer of language cannot be adequately transcribed, so it is often overlooked. A simple "ah" or "oh" may have as many meanings as they have pronunciations. The Hebrews did not write vowels in the earliest times, Herder surmises, because vowels had too many nuances and variations (*SW*, 5:13). Language is oral communication; only later civilizations invented writing systems.

Such natural language, however, is not yet human language. Human beings have weaker senses and instincts than animals. The stronger the senses of animals, the less need these have for language. The human being compensates the lack of adaptive behavior through its capacity for reason (*Vernunftfähigkeit*). This generic difference he calls *Besonnenheit* (*SW*, 5:32). *Besonnenheit* implies memory and reflection. If this is what makes human beings human, language is a natural acquisition; it had to develop in accordance with their human nature. They separated one item from another in the stream of impressions, and by comparing several occurrences, they began to identify characteristic traits. The sheep could be recognized by its bleating sound, and called "the bleating one." Language and reason are bound together: "Without language, man has no reason, and without reason no language" (*SW*, 5:40). This is how Herder answers Süssmilch: the human race could learn language from God only if they possessed reason, because otherwise they would be unable to learn it. If God teaches language as parents teach their children, the analogy is misleading. Children really invent language for themselves when they are ready to learn it (*SW*, 5:41); the parents only help and direct.

Does Herder merely shift the argument? He maintains that human beings are created by God, and as such they must be endowed with the potential for language learning. Herder denies, however, that a direct divine intervention and instruction was needed or possible to develop human language. Thus if humanness implies a potential for reason, the question of the origin of language becomes really irrelevant, however significant the question of the history of languages may be.

Herder sees a parallel between language acquisition in a child and the human race as a whole. This parallelism of ontogenetic and phylogenetic development makes the study of languages doubly significant. Herder's own language theory is inseparable from his anthropology and his philosophy of history.

In a psychological sense, the origin of language is through hearing. Language consists of sounds. For Herder, the sense of hearing is a "middle" sense between seeing and feeling and thus ideal for the understanding of the world. Since actions were the first focus of attention, the first words were verbs, whereas nouns are later derivations. Herder insists on the poetic nature of this early language, which heard the sounds of nature and experienced life in action and motion. Poetry was older than prose (*SW*, 5:56), the first language was singing (5:57). The *sensorium commune* (5:61) in man ensures communication through the unifying sense of feeling. Hearing also keeps a middle ground with respect to the experience of time (5:66).

From a biological point of view, language is a basic need for the slowly developing human species, where children need to be helped and taught by their parents for a long time. Language develops as a response to practical needs and experiences. Thus even if, with Herder (*SW*, 5:134), one assumes a common origin for the human race, and therefore one original language, different needs of different groups will create different languages (5:123–24). In the second part of his *Treatise*, Herder tries to define the anthropological nature of language. Language characterizes an active free-thinking creature (5:93) that moves in groups and is thus in need of communication (5:112). The group character necessarily leads to the development of different national languages (5:123–24). Different conditions create different languages, which in turn determine the way of thinking of a language community. On the premise that language and reason are inseparable, the determining influence of language on thinking and culture is evident.

Herder's *Treatise* has been considered a turning point in language theory and has been much analyzed and commented upon.[16] Herder himself did not claim too much originality but stated that he made free use of ideas that he had found elsewhere.[17] The *Treatise* should not, however, be considered solely in the context of the history of language theory, but also in its significance for Herder's work as a whole. The linkage of reason and language and the determining character of language for man's world view are fundamental points of his philosophy. The *Treatise* has been called psychological,[18] but it is also historical. Herder sketches a cultural history of languages as a sequence of life stages, and he posits the repetition of the history of mankind in each individual human being. The religious aspect is never forgotten. The human being is part of nature, but it is endowed with the potential for reason, which is a divine gift. Language is human, but it is also the medium to receive God's revelation. It is in the earliest poetic and religious documents of mankind that one may come closest to such a revelation.

Thus the *Treatise* contains a nucleus of Herder's future works: his interpretations of Hebrew poetry in the Old Testament, his sensualistic epistemology, and his organicist philosophy of history, as well as his concern for true religion and his insistence on the social and religious meaning of poetry. His sensualistic view of words as verbs has been declared a common trait of the *Sturm und Drang* generation,[19] but it is also characteristic of Herder himself, who distrusted all abstractions and intellectualizations, rejected philosophical system building, and tried to get close to actual sensual experience. Herder objected to the artificiality of philosophical terminology. He himself was always mindful of the sensual derivation of words. *Vernunft* he considered to be derived from *vernehmen* (perceive). The human being first receives sensations and then transforms them into ideas. It is in this context that Herder's often noted shift from the instrumental to the expressive character of language takes place. While clarity and distinctiveness of ideas and their expression are not disdained, they become secondary to the richness of the expression of the "lower faculties" of feeling and sensation in imagery and the music of the language. The ideal is no longer a progressive perfection into mathematics, as Leibniz had envisioned, but a return to the deepest expressive layer of language and human nature. Language has to be learned, and man is a creature that learns. Language is a framework that is never finished but allows for constant change. While *Vervollkommnung* (perfectibility) is the innate nature of this system, its seeming goal, perfection, can never be reached. Imperfection, openness, and striving are part of the human condition.

Albrecht von Haller's famous definition of the human being as a combination of angel and animal is present here in a more sophisticated form. Language is a biological necessity, but also the mark of spirituality. Two seemingly exclusive opposites allow a *coincidentia oppositorum*,[20] a new quality of synthesis. The human being can think with feelings (*SW*, 5:100) and feel with ideas. Language may be both rational and emotional, both poetic and philosophical. And perhaps the impossible, a synthesis of different life stages and different historical ages, can be achieved.

Herder's *Treatise*, a mere sketch, was not to be his last word on language. Language is crucial for his writings on the Bible, for his *Ideas*, and eventually for his critique of Kant. There is not only the line from the *Treatise* to Wilhelm von Humboldt and his followers, but there are also the ramifications into the many different areas of Herder's thinking and writing. Inevitably, thinking for Herder means thinking about language.

Chapter Three
The Bückeburg Achievements
Genesis

Hamann's inspired reading of the Bible had left a deep impression on Herder. In Riga, he accumulated studies on an "archaeology of the Orient." He began to compare different accounts of creation. He wanted to arrive at a better understanding of the Bible. In this effort, he was inspired by Robert Lowth (1710–87) and his Oxford lectures on the sacred poetry of the Hebrews (1753). However, he did not mean to secularize the sacred text or characterize it as "literature." On the contrary, in his opinion, the sacred nature of the text could only be understood through its poetic medium. He also insisted that the Bible was a human document. Without understanding the geography, history, and social organization of Israel and the Orient, one could not arrive at the meaning of the text. Moses, the author of the account of creation, Herder maintained, drew upon an ancient oral tradition that he transformed for his people. One has to retrace his steps to arrive at the earliest and deepest layers. Then one might get close to the beginning of the human race and of religious traditions. Poetry was older than prose, and if God taught man, he would not have taught in discourses, but through images, hints, and signs. Those were *Samenkörner* (seeds) that would grow with the development of the human race and fructify in time. The oldest poetry was thus mythology, the transmission of the creation and the origin of the human race, as it was revealed in divine language.

In this attempt to come closer to the original connection of God and man, Herder discovered the often surprising similarities of the ancient accounts of creation and the beginnings of the human race. Herder's assumption was that they had to have a common source. The evidence available to him was meager, at least compared to today's vast body of knowledge. Thus it was made easier for him to find what he hoped he would find: the "proof" that Genesis, the account of creation in the Old Testament, was the oldest document of the human race. Consequently, Herder called his book *Älteste Urkunde des Menschengeschlechts* (Oldest document of the human race). The book had a multiple purpose. It was commentary on Genesis 1–2; it was to demonstrate the ancient character of the text; and it was to show how God could have instructed the human race. Herder declared emphatically that he would not try to harmonize the account of the Bible with modern science, nor offer a critical or philosophical explanation. He wanted to translate the text to lead to its understanding. In this translation and commentary he made an all-out effort to come close to the monumental simplicity of the original. This was a real *tour de force,* and most critics of Herder, then and later, have declared this experiment a failure.[1] Goethe, however, was deeply impressed, and so was young Jean Paul Richter, who never forgot this impression, which would provide the basis for his lifelong admiration for and friendship with Herder.[2] Herder considered this one of his major works and was shocked by the mostly hostile reception. The reception convinced him to use a more conventional style in the future.

The most apparent stumbling block is certainly the language of this work. In an attempt to get close to the Hebrew original, Herder omits nonessential function words, such as articles and conjunctions; and he tries to intensify the verbal qualities of the words. He also intersperses his commentary with polemics and some boasting. These elements do not mix too well. If Herder had not tried to prove too much, he would have been more convincing.

The creation is symbolized by *Morgenröte* (dawn; the appearance of light). The sun rising for the first time thus becomes much more than the symbol of the appearance of truth. For Herder, God's word that there may be light is the real act of creation. It shows the ultimate identity of deed and word. In the appearance of light, there is the beginning of life, but also simultaneously the beginning of revelation, of truth, and of the enlightenment of the human beings by God.

What was the form of the divine message for the human beings? Herder hit upon the idea of the "hieroglyph." Egyptian script had not yet been deciphered; accordingly, the word *hieroglyph* should not be understood in a technical sense. It simply meant a complex pictorial symbol for a meaningful message. A hieroglyph would be characterized by the unity of form and content, by monumental simplicity, and all-embracing substance. The fundamental hieroglyphs would express the seven days of creation as well as its fundamental elements, thus symbolizing the order and nature of the world. Herder arrived at the following basic word picture: (*SW*, 6:292):

I

LIGHT

II   III

HEAVEN   EARTH

(high)   (low)

IV

LIGHTS:

Sun and Moon

V   VI

CREATURES   CREATURES

OF HEAVEN   OF THE EARTH

(Water, Air)

VII

Sabbath

In a letter from Strassburg, Herder had given it this abstract form in the Greek alphabet:[3]

A

H   E

I

O   Y

W

In both cases, the form is that of two triangles joined, or a hexagon with a point at its center. The central vertical axis is that of light separating the high heaven from the low earth. From this basic design, Herder was able to arrive at many modifications, all of them demonstrating the order of the universe under different aspects and names.

This divine message in hieroglyphs is the communication of general ideas, but in form of living images rather than concepts. The hieroglyphs have to be grasped immediately and intuitively, and this would be the appropriate way of understanding early mythology and its divine messages. Like Kant, Herder rejects all intellectual proofs for God's existence. But where Kant declares faith in God to be purely subjective, Herder presents evidence of God's existence. This is evidence not for the intellect, but for the senses and for intuition. A re-creation of the process of creation and of the original communication between God and human beings pierces through the intellectual shell of the philosophical age and opens up deeper layers. The ultimate object of Herder's often praised historical *Einfühlung*, empathy and intuition, is the biblical text, especially Genesis.

Herder was never content with stating a hypothesis. He wanted to prove the truth, and he adduced as much empirical evidence as he could find, interpreted in his morphological and psychohistorical manner. Thus he ventured far into the field of comparative religion and mythology, pointing out similarities in Oriental, especially Persian, and Egyptian accounts of creation. He may have been wrong in details, but he certainly paved the way for future studies.[4] Also, Herder's search for the beginnings, for the origin of man and language, gave a powerful signal to German romantics in their search for the original unity of the human race. Herder himself was to locate man's original habitat in northern India, and thus pointed to the central importance of Indian culture.[5] He adhered, however, to his thesis of the *Oldest Document* that made Genesis the source for all accounts of creation.

Herder, who lived in considerable isolation in Bückeburg, had misjudged his audience. He was not going to change his message, but he retreated from stylistic experiments. He would sow his seeds through allusions, metaphors, examples, and allegories within the framework of reasoned discourse. He even called his *Ideas* a mere restatement of the *Oldest Document*,[6] although this must be taken with a grain of salt. Thus Herder was forced into a compromise with his philosophically and scientifically minded age.

Herder's insistence on creation and the essential truth of the biblical text seems to be in contradiction with his evolutionist approach that has even been linked to Darwin.[7] The key to that seeming contradiction may lie in another idea of evolution: the evolution of the forms of human knowledge. The biblical text is a text for early man, and the early human mind's way of grasping the truth. Many variations of the story of creation can be understood in the light of specific historical conditions. Still, they are all part of the one universal truth, which appears in so many different forms, as human beings are imperfect and have only limited access to the sources of knowledge. Herder believed in the original unity and subsequent separation of the human race, from God and from each other. He found a universal truth of divine revelation in all forms of religion, although he believed in the superior virtues of Christianity over other religions. Nevertheless, the ultimate hope for a reunification of the human race clearly motivated the search for its beginnings.

The *Oldest Document* is a hybrid of poetry and prose. It shows ambiguities in Herder's approach and possibly the limits of his talent and his perspective. Herder, like Luther, wanted to find his way to the original word of God, but he found himself alienated in a modern world ruled by abstract philosophies. The style of the *Oldest Document* is not quite as opaque as it is reported to be, and the work is not an irrationalist statement but a statement defining the limits of reason and pointing to forms of truth outside of rationalism. Herder struggles with the heritage of Luther and the Enlightenment. This forced synthesis may make the contradictions more visible than their supposed unity, but it turned out to be a seminal experiment nevertheless.

A New Philosophy of History

In 1774, the year of the *Oldest Document,* Herder published a sketch of a universal history with the defiant title *Auch eine Philosophie der Geschichte zur Bildung der Menschheit* (Another philosophy of history for the formation of Humankind). The oppositional nature of the book is underscored by the subtitle "Beytrag zu vielen Beyträgen des Jahrhunderts" (Contribution to many contributions of the century), plus the motto from Epictetus, which says that man is not disturbed or confused by facts, *pragmata,* but by opinions, *dogmata,* about the facts. Obviously, Herder intended a critique of critiques. He added his critical view to demonstrate the limitations of his century. Friedrich Meinecke has hailed this sketch as Herder's major achievement, the beginning of real historical thinking.[8] Inevitably, most scholars compare this short draft of little over one hundred pages (*SW,* 5:475–586) with Herder's central work, the *Ideas,* and find it wanting. *Another Philosophy,* however, is merely a pamphlet, a manifesto, the first sounding of a new call. It is anything but a finished work.

The work has three sections, of which the first has left the deepest impression on posterity. It contains the best-known elements of Herder's philosophy of history. Herder begins by postulating "the origin of the whole race" (*SW*, 5:477) from "one human couple," as in the biblical story. Together with his recurrence to the Bible, Herder insists on the analogy of historical and natural processes: "It is natural that these first developments were as simple, delicate, and wonderful as we see them in all productions of nature" (5:477). His fundamental example is the seed, the germ that falls into the earth and is developed there without anybody's notice. The real beginnings of everything are always in the dark. The subsequent way of human civilization from the *Morgenland* (Orient) to Egypt, Greece, and Rome is seen as analogous to the life stages of humans: childhood, youth, and maturity. Herder cautions himself against undue generalizations: "Nobody in the world feels more than I do the weakness of general characterization" (5:501). Human beings are individuals, peoples and ages are abstractions. They follow each other like the waves in the sea. Still, Herder argues on the basis of a certain anthropology. Human beings have to learn; they are formed (*gebildet*) and progress through learning. Each civilization, like each individual, is striving for perfection. There is a *kairos*, a climax for each culture and individual, an optimal state of harmony of conditions and abilities, a state of happiness. Happiness, however, is reached in very different ways by different ages. It would be foolish to judge history from the point of view of eighteenth-century ideals.

Herder's analogy between history and the life stages of the individual human being seemed to work best for ancient history. The developmental cycles of post-Roman history that Herder presented in his second section are not quite as clear. However, he emphasized the overriding idea of palingenesis in history, of the renewal after the death of ancient civilization, a renewal brought about by Christianity—a flower from the old civilization—and the new peoples from the north of Europe. The Middle Ages, for Herder, are by no means "dark ages." All ages must be understood from their intrinsic values and aspirations.

Herder tries to explain how change comes about in history. Small causes start great movements. New movements have to find their way into reality against violent and stubborn opposition. The history of nature and of the human race is one of revolutions (*SW*, 5:532). "Revolution" was a term from astronomy beginning to take on its new political meaning when Herder was writing.[9] "Revolution" was a cyclical process, like the revolution of the planets around the sun. Although it may be violent, revolution in history is not chaos, it is rather a sign of continuity and order, and above all of vitality.

Herder strongly objected to the "mechanical spirit" (SW, 5:534), that tranforms everything into a machine. A machine can be guided by one person (5:534); it results in a division of head and hand. The state as a machine is a dictatorship where everybody except the guiding spirit is reduced to a cog or a tool. *Bildung,* Herder emphasizes, should happen through many sources and media, and cannot really be controlled. A society, just like an individual, must be *gebildet,* from natural conditions, past history, social customs, through fate, chance, or some specific influences. Instead of trying to rule the world through the intellect, it should be left to grow according to its striving for perfection.

Herder's criticism of his own age is as sharp as that of Rousseau, but there are essential differences.[10] Both writers try to change the direction of history away from the grand design of rationalism. Herder attacks the "philosophical" spirit of his age, by which he means its rationalism. He himself overrules the obvious objection that it is easy to be impartial and tolerant toward past ages and far-away cultures, but that one is too much involved in one's own time to be fair (SW,5:545). He points to the brutality of colonial empires with their destruction of native cultures, to modern engines of war. He sees little benefit for humanity in the system of balance of powers prevailing in Europe, and he does not approve of the European system of trade that robs other continents. In general, he is critical of the European way of life and not impressed by the state of the arts and sciences. He does not even want to discuss religion (5:553–54). Obviously, the eighteenth century is not for Herder the apex of progress in history, but an age of crisis, ready for a revolution.

Herder's third section consists of addenda. These thirty pages of footnotes should not be dismissed, as they present a number of points dear to Herder's heart. Among them is a point that also bothered Kant and Lessing: if history is progress from lower to higher forms of life, and from lesser to greater happiness, how could such a sacrifice of earlier people for the later ones be morally justified? Lessing, in his *Education of Mankind,* thought of the idea of reincarnation. Herder, although he was intrigued by that possibility, believed in a balance of happiness for each age. *Schicksal* (fate), which governs history, is equitable. It gives and takes. Each progress brings as much loss as it brings gains. The modern age has dramatically changed the relationship between the individual and society; ancient heroes and geniuses would not be possible today. Socrates and Aristotle could not live in the eighteenth century.

For Herder, the eighteenth century is an age of extremes. The global nature of the economy and of politics has transformed cultures that previously moved in small spheres: "It is almost inevitable that the higher and more expansive character of our century will result in ambiguities of the *best* and *worst* actions, which would not take place in narrower and lower spheres" (*SW*, 5:580–81). Instead of many small cultures and states, with smaller virtues and vices, the large dimensions of modern world culture bring with them extremes of greatness and depravity. Yet Herder still expects the better to prevail; he is looking forward to improvement and perfectibility. As change cannot come from the governing mediocrities, extraordinary human beings will have to disturb the order, like comets in the heavens (5:584).

In his concluding *peroratio*, Herder offers an *Aussicht* on history as a whole. If one could see the history of humankind together, he assumes, the laws of history would be evident, and the order of creation would be revealed. But one's lowly *Endpunkt* (*SW*, 5:584), with its limitations and many sources of error, mandates a posture of humility, although one might dream about the grand vision. There is not much as yet, however, that we are able to read in the book of God (5:585).

Religion is thus the beginning and the end of this philosophy of history. Most significant is the organicist model of development, always present in Herder's constant metaphors of trees, flowers, and seeds. If the individual is seen as an organism, it is unique and must be allowed to grow and take its own shape. At the same time, it is part of an interdependent environment, of a chain of beings, where life is generated and sustained through give and take and mutual recognition. Thus in a society based on the forces of tradition and environmental conditions, each individual has something to contribute and is therefore significant.

It is anything but easy to transfer such ideal terms to the structure of modern differentiated societies, as they seem to correspond more to the simpler forms of older societies. The consequences for Germany of the idea of the state as an organism have not been very good—to say the least.[11] Herder sought an alternative to the power-hungry and totally artificial absolutist states that were based on mechanistic models. The state as a machine dehumanizes, he thought, whereas a community seen as an organism would respect its constituent members. The fundamental difference between Herder's views and that of later "organicists" is that they did not respect, as he did, the uniqueness and independence of individuals. On the contrary, they saw them merely as "organs."

With Herder's approach, history cannot be treated as a sequence of rulers, wars, and political actions. Human history is not that of individuals, but that of civilizations and the change of periods. A few individuals may make a real difference, but the main forces of history—whether spiritual, economic, environmental, or biological—are collective. History has become cultural history in a very broad sense. Above all, there is still the striving for perfectibility, which is an innate law of natural beings, but propels humanity toward the divine. Without God, the meaning of history would be very much in doubt.

Another Philosophy defies the claim of the eighteenth century that progress has been achieved. Herder sees balance and change in history instead of linear progress. Every "progress" implies a loss. Mankind has to recognize the limitations of its condition. There is no way to combine the blessings of ancient idyllic life and modern civilization.

When Herder was asked by his publisher to prepare a second edition of *Another Philosophy*, he realized that he had changed too much to be happy with the often strident tone of this long essay. In order to convince rather than persuade, he sat down and provided the wealth of evidence that was missing in this sketch. Thus the *Ideas,* while starting from the same point of departure, are a work of a different nature. In a way, just as *Another Philosophy* was a critique of Herder's predecessors, the *Ideas* are not only a continuation but also a critique of the earlier work.

German Art

Herder had a single publisher, his friend Johann Friedrich Hartknoch, in Riga, and he remained loyal to him, although the temperamental Karoline occasionally complained about financial conditions. But there were special cases. The publisher Bode in

Hamburg had issued the *Literaturbriefe,* edited by Heinrich Wilhelm von Gerstenberg (1737–1823), who is best known for his writings on Shakespeare and Nordic poetry and for his tragedy *Ugolino,* enthusiastically reviewed by Herder. Bode tried to keep the *Literaturbriefe* alive without Gerstenberg and hoped for Herder's help. Herder had written a review on the translations of *Ossian* and was working on an essay on Shakespeare. But the journal could not be revived, and when Herder realized that Bode wanted to publish Herder's essays as a separate book, Herder considered them too insignificant. Instead he brought together a collection of five items by combining his essays with a piece by Goethe on Gothic art. As a counterpoint, he added the translation of an Italian essay on Gothic style by a man named Frisi. He rounded it out with the introduction of Justus Möser to his history of Osnabrück, called *Deutsche Geschichte.* It was more a burden of duty than a labor of love, and Herder was apologetic about the little volume, especially when it was badly printed and had a large number of printing errors and other flaws. [12] It was not reprinted, and the editors of Herder's collected works treated the volume with some neglect. It was much later that Germanists elevated it to the rank of a manifesto for a new era of German art and literature. One of the reasons for that may have been the catchy title *Von deutscher Art und Kunst* (Of German kind and art). Herder himself subtitled it apologetically "Einige fliegende Blätter" (some flying leaves).

In spite of Herder's cavalier attitude about the collection, it may have been a more influential publication than even the *Oldest Document* or *Another Philosophy.* The attribute "German" is crucial here. Goethe called the Gothic style "German art," Möser wrote on "German history," and even Shakespeare and Ossian enter into this "German" context. Gerstenberg had advocated the reorientation of German culture from the correctness and conventionality of Latin cultural influences toward the presumed genuineness and individuality of Northern European literature, English, and Scandinavian. Herder, who was less one-sided, since he extolled the beauties of Hebrew poetry and Homer's Greece, still agreed, as he was in search of poetic expressions of a true national spirit. This attracted him to MacPherson's *Ossian,* and he found in it traits of ancient folk poetry, so that he considered it a true document of ancient Scotland. MacPherson had indeed to be skillful enough to reproduce the style of folk songs, the Bible, and Homer. Herder persisted in believing

Ossian to be genuine, although the evidence of its fabrication was mounting. Herder's letters on *Ossian* discuss the strengths and weaknesses of the German translation by Denis, but also defend its ancient character. The real point of the essay, however, is not *Ossian* at all, but the discussion of the nature of folk songs, with a good number of examples from various languages, mostly in Herder's own translations. These are samples from Herder's collection of folk songs and a new source of inspiration for future poets. Herder criticizes the Denis translation for trying to "elevate" Ossian to the level of eighteenth-century civilization, instead of rendering the true primitivism of the original, with all its vitality and genuineness, as Herder tries to do in his translations of folk songs. Goethe's *Heidenröslein,* which figures in all of Herder's collections of true German folk art, may have been the first fruit of this inspiration, which was to be crucial for German romanticism.

Herder's essay on Shakespeare reads like a work in progress and would not have been published without his obligations to Bode.[13] In this essay Herder tries to find his own ground between the interpretations of Gerstenberg and Lessing. Herder's main point is that the rules of drama and theater depend on the historical and cultural conditions of the age and country. Shakespeare could not possibly have written Greek tragedies. Herder stressed the individuality of Shakespeare's style; he saw his "irregularities" as virtues. He thus created the nineteenth-century German image of Shakespeare as the lonely genius. At the same time, Herder, disregarding the artifices of his style, stressed the nearness of Shakespeare to folk art. For Herder Shakespeare's historical plays represent a true synthesis of poetry and history, and of the social and the individual. He considered Shakespeare close to German art, as had Lessing before him, and thus a true model for a future drama. In spite of some reservations, the first Shakespearian play on German history, Goethe's *Götz von Berlichingen,* was welcomed by Herder as an auspicious beginning.[14]

Herder's way of experiencing Shakespeare, his praise of folk songs, Goethe's enthusiasm for mediaeval German art, specifically architecture, and Möser's insistence on regional traditions as a source for a renewal of the German nation were well received by the young generation of the day. In spite of early patriotic excesses, especially among the students in Göttingen, this call for a return to popular traditions was healthy and one of the wellsprings of the German cultural achievements around 1800. Herder did not value this volume too much, as his main concerns were elsewhere; but it somehow took on a life of its own.

Theology

In Bückeburg Herder became for the first time a church official, albeit one of a very neglected and provincial church. He never found a true line of communication with his parishioners, and he was caught between the enlightened absolutism of his prince and the mindless orthodoxy prevailing in the country. He could not expect to find partners who, like him, would side with Lessing in his theological quarrels and who had his ecumenical outlook.[15] Still, there was a real reason why Herder, contrary to so many contemporary writers and former students of theology, devoted his life to the Lutheran Church.[16] With his liberal views that might even now shock devout and orthodox Lutherans,[17] Herder considered it his duty to work for the improvement of the church. No wonder that while in Bückeburg he began publishing in the field of religion.

The Bückeburg period is the first stage of Herder's concerted efforts in this field. The works of the early Weimar period, such as *The Spirit of Hebrew Poetry*, may be considered a continuation of the Bückeburg momentum. Only late in life, with the so-called "Christian Writings" of the 1790s, did Herder return to religious issues with such an intensity.

Herder's Bückeburg writings are generally considered to reflect a change from the liberal attitudes typical of the Riga years to a deeper religiosity, a return to pietistic traditions. Sometimes, the influence of Hamann is thought to be responsible for this change, but biographically, this assumption is difficult to uphold. Herder and Hamann were close during the Riga years, but after their serious disagreements on the question of the origin of language, their correspondence had stopped during the early Bückeburg years. Herder did not need outside influences. His intense attention to church duties, combined with the unexpected experience of social failure, brought him back to an internalized faith. Herder's "break with the Enlightenment," as it has been called,[18] signaled by his irreconcilable differences with Friedrich Nicolai, does not imply new attitudes, but simply a stronger affirmation of views already held before. In the same manner, Herder would lean more toward "Enlightenment" views in a different environment and under different historical circumstances. In spite of the *Sturm und Drang* mannerisms of the Bückeburg years, there is a surprising continuity in Herder's work and thinking.

It is somewhat of a misnomer to call Herder's writings on religion "theological." The theological faculty at the University of Göttingen knew better. They voiced objections to Herder, not only because of his questionable orthodoxy, but also because he was not a real theologian. Indeed, Herder saw his role as a mediator for his readers to gain access to the biblical text. He used the critical tools available to him for a better translation and exegesis. He approached the Bible as a divinely inspired book written for humans by humans.

The second group of Bückeburg writings in the area of religion deals with the proper functions of a minister. His *An Prediger. Fünfzehn Provinzialblätter* (For preachers: fifteen provincial letters, 1774) reflects his negative experiences in Bückeburg. Following Pascal's famous example, the tone of these letters is polemical, even vehement at times. Herder attacked Johann Joachim Spalding, one of the most prominent and respected Lutheran ministers in Germany. He criticized Spalding's admired moderation[19] which was once more demonstrated by his recent and popular book on the usefulness of preaching. Herder respected Spalding as a person and as a writer, but he was disgusted with the lukewarm attitude of ministers. Why should the church be so meek and merely ask for an indifferent tolerance of the state? Although theologians like Lavater and—later—Schleiermacher admired Spalding, Herder was fed up with too much accommodation and compromise on the part of the Lutheran church. Although a minister is appointed by the state authorities, Herder felt, he is still the prophet of God and responsible to a higher master than his secular ruler. He should not water down his sermons to mere benevolent moral lessons, as Spalding seemed to advocate.

To prove his point, Herder included a short history of preaching and the role of preachers. In fact, he mounted a counterattack against the ubiquitous condemnation of "priests" by the Enlightenment. The minister is the mediator of truth, not lies; and Herder appealed to the shining example of Martin Luther. More than that: *"Philosophy of Mankind,* and its *true history*—none except a priest of God will write it one day, will add new pages by writing it; at present, the swampy source has neither bottom nor edge" (*SW,* 7:300). History is made by writing it, but in the "philosophical age," the source for historical truth is not a revelation from above, but only an impure imagination. History cannot be written unless with a mind filled with good thoughts, or a divine inspiration. The connection with Herder's other books of that year is evident, as is the need for explaining the symbolic books of the Bible in their historicity. History and revelation are not contradictions, but different yet interdependent spheres. The understanding of history leads to more than relative truths.

It is noteworthy that Herder agrees with Spalding in the rejection of zealots and false enthusiasts (Schwärmer), especially those of the pietist variety. The church is rooted in society, but it should be respected for its higher truth and wisdom, not merely tolerated as an instrument for maintaining public morality. Herder admonishes ministers to have more self-respect, courage, conviction, and independence. Ultimately, the preacher is a prophet. Society, according to Herder, does not arise through a social contract (*SW*, 7:294), but develops from family groups, that is, groups with natural bonds and natural leaders who would be their priests or kings. Priesthood and its wisdom are based on a long oral tradition as summarized in the Bible. The ancient dignity of a priest is fundamentally different from the "civil priest" (*SW*, 7:295) of the present age, who "gains" his office through marriage or protection, who has no real calling for the ministry and is afraid of offending his patron(s).

Herder continued the *Oldest Document* beyond Genesis. The second part appeared in 1776. It concentrated on the biblical account of the creation of man, Adam and Eve, and their fall, but did not stop there. In trying to explain the original text in its simplicity, and in commonsense terms of geography and history, Herder saw the inevitability of the fall in the imperfection of human nature as well as its positive consequences as a challenge for future perfection. He wanted the original story to be simple and "natural." Again, Herder found Oriental, specifically Persian, sources as parallels of the biblical stories.[20] His vision of the Bible, especially of Christianity, was heavily influenced by St. John's first chapter in the Gospels, and his message of universal love.

In this context it is understandable that he tried to come to grips with St. John's revelation of the end of the world and the Last Judgment. After long labors,[21] including a poetic translation of the text, Herder finally published his commentary as *Maran Atha: Das*

Buch von der Zukunft des Herrn, des Neuen Testaments Siegel (Maran Atha: the book of the future of the Lord, the seal of the New Testament), in 1779. In spite of the late date, it is still a characteristic product of the Bückeburg period, written with the pious Countess Maria in mind. Herder makes great efforts to stay away from all semblance of mysticism. He points out how many seemingly startling images of the text are taken from everyday life and the language of the Orient. He considers the text in its cultural and historical ambience. He draws parallels to other parts of the Bible and adduces linguistic evidence from modern Oriental languages. He makes it a point to understand the text without recourse to esoteric or mystical knowledge. This explanation, like the other commentaries of Herder, wants to document the faith and vision of the first Christians, those who had known Jesus in person or through his disciples. They were human beings, and their human wisdom and views should be understood.

"Understanding" of the Bible is for Herder still identical with a conviction of its truth. God's message to man, as he never tired of saying, did not take the form of moral discourse, but that of *Samenkörner* (seeds) (*SW*, 7:242) that would be pregnant with many things. The Bible is a human document about the interaction of God and man, man receiving the divine message in symbols and images, without necessarily understanding it. The hieroglyph and the holy number 7 reappear in Herder's commentaries. The *Oldest Document* demonstrates this approach with its Genesis commentary, but the entire biblical text is equally a human document of divine inspiration, presented in the form of a poetic history. Herder is mindful of the linguistic identity of story and history in the German word *Geschichte*. Myths and legends are stories, but accounts of history nonetheless. *Geschichte* can be a fundamental term for any account of what happened, irrespective of its level of symbolism and its kind of documentation.

Herder's writings of the Bückeburg period seemed to address a small group of believers rather than a general and largely skeptical public. This changed again after his move to Weimar. While in Bückeburg, he had felt close to the zealous Johann Kaspar Lavater (1741–1801) from Zürich; but he soon lost touch with him and renewed his ties with Lessing and Goethe. Herder's fundamental beliefs and objectives, however, never changed.

Herder's theological writings are really "antitheological," since they attempt to cut through modern criticism and dogma in order to find the way back to the Bible text itself. Although Herder never disdains the help of this criticism, he is afraid that it has become an end in itself, instead of a tool, and thus would be a hindrance rather than a help for a Christian. Most of all, Herder opposes dogmatism. Dogma separates and divides, whereas religion unites, humanity. Religion can take many forms, which may be justified under the given circumstances. Christianity remains for Herder the ideal religion, but not as an exclusive fanaticism. Herder would never give up the eighteenth-century message of happiness, tolerance, and progress of true *Humanität*. However, he saw this process not as a liberation from religion, but as a liberation for true religion.

Prize Essays

Herder wrote a great number of essays for prize competitions of various academies, including a Latin essay for a French competition.[22] He won three prizes in Berlin: in 1771, 1773, and 1780. He did not win the Berlin prize in 1774 and 1775 with his versions of *On the Cognition and Sensation of the Human Soul*. He also won two prizes from the Bavarian Academy of Sciences, in 1778 and 1779. He did not win in Göttingen and Kassel. There are other essays he conceived in connection with such competitions, but did not submit. This activity continued through the seventies, but it may be discussed here at the end of the Bückeburg period.

It seems surprising that Herder, who was critical of German governments, especially that of his native Prussia and its famous King Frederick II, and who was rather hostile to the universities of his day, would crave official recognition with such tenacity. More strikingly still, some of his responses were obviously ironical and almost a mockery of the question and the institution. And yet Herder wanted the recognition, and in Prussia, he really desired to be elected member of the academy—a goal he attained only in 1787, after the death of Frederick II. Herder was thus neither recognized by nor reconciled with the great king.

The German universities of this period, with a few notable exceptions such as Göttingen, were in dire need of reform. The economic pressure that students had to attend their state universities to have their degrees recognized, had resulted in the creation of a large number of universities without much vitality.[23] Therefore,

reform-minded rulers had founded academies of science for the promotion of scholarship and freer discussion. Some of them, however,
turned out to be playthings of the rulers, and the political and
economic restrictions typical for the period were evident in all cases.
Still, there was reason to hope, as Herder did, for their use as a
vehicle for the discussion of relevant issues, especially educational
reforms. It was no accident that in 1787 the liberal Margrave Karl
Friedrich of Baden asked Herder to draw up a plan for a "German
Academy," a plan fitting into the context of the *Fürstenbund,* the
last attempt to reform and save the crumbling German *Reich.* Herder
responded with a *Plan zum ersten patriotischen Institut für den Allgemeingeist Deutschlands* (Plan for the first patriotic institute for the
general spirit of Germany). The plan never materialized. It would
have cost too much money, according to Herder's Duke Karl August. Poverty and fragmentation precluded any meaningful planning
for the future.

Most of the prize essays deal with aspects of the social functions
of the arts and sciences, including the role of government in the
field of culture. Herder's real intentions are revealed by the fact that
these "academic" writings are not at all academic in style and content. The most academic of them was *Wie die deutschen Bischöfe
Landstände wurden* (How the German bishops became an estate of
the realm), written in 1774 for Göttingen, but neither recognized
by a prize nor printed. The essay belongs in the context of the
Provincial Letters. It clearly objects to the increasing political function
and power of the bishops in the Middle Ages, and thus can be taken
as a plea for more separation of church and state. The church,
concerned with political matters, forgets about her real duties. In
this essay, Herder treats history as a "natural doctrine of succession"
(*SW,* 5:679) and avoids moralizing. However, it is clear that he
does more than just retell a particular development. He interprets
history.

The titles of the major prize essays show their close interconnections. In 1773, he discussed the *Ursachen des gesunknen Geschmacks
bei den verschiedenen Völkern, da er geblühet* (Causes of the decadence
of taste in the various nations where it once flourished). In 1778,
he dealt with *Ueber die Würkung der Dichtkunst auf die Sitten der Völker
in alten und neuen Zeiten* (On the effects of poetry on the customs of
the peoples in old and modern times). In 1779 he wrote *Ueber den
Einfluss der schönen in die höheren Wissenschaften* (On the influence of

the humanities on the higher sciences), and in 1780 *Ueber den Einfluss der Regierung auf die Wissenschaften und der Wissenschaften auf die Regierung* (On the influence of government on the sciences and of the sciences on government). These essays have more in common than content matter. They discuss a specific thesis and provide evidence in the form of short historical surveys. They are concise and stimulating, but do not attempt to be exhaustive or profound. Herder tries to prove his major thesis that the arts and sciences flourish when they are in harmony with the aspirations of the entire nation and address general concerns. In comparison with ancient Greece and Rome, a decadence of taste was generally recognized and deplored for eighteenth-century Germany. Herder shows that it cannot be changed by government *fiat*. There is no contradiction between genius and good taste. Taste can only arise where a genius has already created great art. Taste only orders and classifies. If a work of genius shows a deficiency in taste, it is a healthy sign for a young rising culture. The length of a creative period of a given culture depends on the "depth" of the culture. A creative age sustained only by a small aristocratic class, as in Augustus's Rome and in Louis XIV's France, cannot last long.

With all attempted fairness to monarchies and enlightened rulers, the republican spirit is clearly most conducive to art or real genius and public significance. Critical and satirical literature belongs to ages of decay, Herder maintains, and for him the function of the arts in a rising society is positive and affirmative. He utterly comdemns creative works that are a mere flattery of powerful persons or are wholly private in nature. There should be no art for art's sake. Art is part of human existence. It is not ethics, but it cannot be separated from the moral values in its depiction of the human condition as a whole.

The arguments for the proper study of the humanities have changed very little over the last two centuries. Herder's concept of *schöne Wissenschaften* includes literature, the arts, and philosophy. He argues that these *schöne Wissenschaften* do not only provide the general educational background needed for professional studies, but also a necessary human development. The arts—whose main concern was with the "lower" faculties, that is, emotion and the senses—were needed as an antidote against false intellectualization and the atrophy of the human personality.

In Herder's day, governments interfered with a heavy hand in the pursuit of the sciences. Herder admitted that the sciences—including the humanities—were a social concern and thus a legitimate area for government involvement. But government should provide support, encouragement, and freedom, and not try to give directions. Government and science represent the same social spirit and thus reinforce each other. Their interdependence should not be seen in merely utilitarian terms. Herder argued for *Gedankenfreiheit* (*SW*, 9:357), allowing scholars and philosophers to think, work, and express their ideas, even to be involved in social affairs, if their research warranted it. Science can have a civilizing effect on society. However, nature is stronger than regulations. "Each state has its period of growth, of maintaining itself, and of decay, and this determines its sciences and arts" (9:375).

The academies were a public forum, although for a very limited public. Herder could hope to reach at least some responsible people with his appeals. His message calls, most of all, for freedom. Not any form of art, nor science even, can be nurtured artificially. It has to grow from "seeds" in their environment of the entire nation. Thus government, the arts and sciences, and the social life of the community are indivisible. No individual ruler could or should regulate the creative spirit of the people. Herder does not touch on specific German conditions of his time, and for good reasons. He could not say what he would have liked to say. But by implication his conclusions are clear. One feels, moreover, that there was a first stirring of public opinion in Germany, and that exciting events were happening, such as the American War of Independence and the shameful sale of German soldiers to England (*SW*, 8:434). Literature responds to the time: "Give us different times, different customs, different male and female readers, different literature educating these readers, and poetry will not resist them" (8:433). Herder openly deplored the lack of an *Allgemeingeist,* a general spirit, and a public forum in Germany. He wanted his essays to contribute to the formation of such a spirit. These are messages both to the academies themselves, urging them to become more progressive and relevant, and to the general public. In this sense, they are still contributions to the great movement of the Enlightenment.

Chapter Four
The Weimar Synthesis
Epistemology

In contrast to his teacher Kant, Herder was never seriously bothered by epistemological problems. Kant's demolition of traditional metaphysics in his *Critique of Pure Reason* did not effect Herder as it did Friedrich Heinrich Jacobi, Jean Paul Richter, or Heinrich von Kleist. The basic reason for this was that it did not occur to Herder to entertain the thought of doubting the existence of God. God was for Herder the *Pantokrator,* the *Allerhalter,* the spirit giving life and order to the universe. Herder's early development shows no period of skepticism, no existential uncertainty. His word on human cognition has thus to be seen in the context of his fight against one-sided intellectualism. It is a short essay with the title *Vom Erkennen und Empfinden der menschlichen Seele* (On the cognition and sensation of the human soul) with the characteristic subtitle "Remarks and Dreams," published in 1778. It had passed through several stages, beginning with a prize essay of 1774 that was rejected. *On the Cognition and Sensation* has been little noticed by philosophers and psychologists, but it is certainly an important statement.

The short work (*SW,* 8:169–235) is divided into two *Versuche* (essays). The first is called "On Cognition and Sensation in their Human Origin and the Laws of the Effects." Herder follows Albrecht von Haller (1708–77) in his basic thesis that man does not know the inner forces of nature. According to Herder, all that we know of nature is in analogy to human nature. This analogy can yield human truth, and that is the only truth accessible to us. This emphatic statement (8:170) shows Herder's closeness to Kant. Cognition of the laws of nature depends on the structure of the human mind. There is truth in this analogy, if it can be assumed that the human mind reflects the divine order of the universe and its unity in diversity. Since Herder posits the reality of God's creation, he is spared Kant's vexing problem, that is, the dichotomy of phenomena versus the "thing in itself" that the human mind will never be able to resolve and know. For Herder, knowledge of reality can be attained in spite of the limited faculties of the human being. However, Dante, Homer, and Shakespeare provide more convincing evidence for man's nature and place in the universe than syllogisms of philosophers (8:171).

Taking Albrecht von Haller's work on physiology as his guide, Herder takes his departure from physiological sources, muscles and nerves. He posits a basic form of stimulation *(Reiz)* and finds it at work everywhere in organic nature, especially in the animal world. Herder insists on living forces in nature, particularly, the concept of *Kraft* (force), although he cannot explain what *Kraft* really is and how it functions. Deploring the lack of data in empirical psychology, he points to three potential sources for psychological data: autobiographies; observations of physicians and friends; and the intuition of writers *(SW,* 8:180). He relies on observation of oneself, observation of others, and on the generalizations that a person of genius can make on the basis of such observations.

Herder agrees with the Leibnizian approach[1] that sees a gradual progression from "dark," that is, subconscious, forces to consciousness and self-consciousness. He argues against the Wolffian school of psychology with its rigid classifications and separation of faculties. Instead of separate *Vermögen,* the fundamental unity of cognition and sensation needs to be emphasized.

The human physio-psychological system is set in motion through the senses. The soul could not project an inner world to the outside. Stimulation through the senses is basic *(SW,* 8:193). Herder largely ignores the eighteenth-century problem of body and soul by defining them as one interacting unit that should not even be separated conceptually. Then he describes, in Leibnizian terms, the rise of consciousness. Sensations rising to a certain level of *Helle* (lucidity) become apperception, thought, and "the soul recognizes that it perceives" (8:193). *Gedanke* (thought) is not defined. It has the power to make *ein lichtes Eins* (a lucid One) of the many things perceived. Thought also causes a *Rückwürkung* (reaction), leading to a feeling of self, oneness, and identity (8:194). This self is not the Neoplatonic mirror creating out of itself (8:194);[2] it remains dependent on the stimulation from the outside world through the senses. The medium of the consciousness of our feeling of self (8:195) is language. No cognition occurs without language, and vice versa. Word and reason are from one source, as indicated by expressions in older languages such as *logos* (8:197). Cognition as apperception, consciousness of self, is necessarily connected with willing. Feeling of self is at the same time *Mitgefühl* (feeling with others) (8:199). Cognition is active and social. In its highest form it becomes love, as was stated by St. John and Spinoza (8:202).

In his second *Versuch*, Herder examines the "influence of both forces on each other and on the character and genius of the human being." Thinking depends on feeling, and feeling receives influences from thinking. There is always interaction of two seemingly opposite forces. In general, there is a cyclical process of expansion and contraction, from physiological to mental processes. Human nature demands a unity of opposites; sensation and cognition joined together (*SW*, 8:233). There is no *reines Denken* (pure thinking). That very idea is *Schwärmerei*, an impossible dream. The knowledge of immortality is beyond human capabilities. True religion must be active and in thoughts, not in mere dreaming and feeling.

As usual, Herder ends with an *Aussicht* into religion, but the essay itself insists on the psychosomatic unity of the human being. In his idea of vital forces and his sensualism, Herder's staked out in advance a counterposition to Kant's *Critique*. He rejected the very notion of Kant's "pure reason"[3] and maintained his empiricist links between sensation and cognition. It would still be unfair to call Herder merely a *Gefühlsphilosoph*, as has been done so many times. Herder and many of his German contemporaries were familiar with English empiricism, and its influence may go deeper than German idealists have wanted to acknowledge.[4]

For the 1775 version of the essay, Herder had developed an incipient characterology. He applied expansion and contraction to psychological types of *Ausbreitung* and *Innigkeit* (expansiveness and inwardness) (*SW*, 8:309). The inward type has few, but intense feelings: inwardness, concentration in a limited sphere, means strong action in one specific point. The expansive mind is adaptable to different situations and does many things at once. The inward mood is with oneself, the outward mood with the object. This idea of introversion and extroversion has become familiar to the twentieth century; for Herder, it may have looked too speculative.

On the Cognition and Sensation is a short essay that hides some of its empiricist positions behind Leibnizian terminology. It is an important statement of Herder's anthropology, and as such contains ideas that inform his better known works. It shows Herder moving in an opposite direction from Kant, indicating that Kantianism was not the only intellectual trend of the period.

Plastic Arts

Plastik (Plastic arts), a little book of 1778, had its beginnings early in Herder's career, certainly in Riga. His stay in Paris provided him with firsthand knowledge of original statues. The fourth, unpublished "grove" of the *Critical Forests* touches on these problems. A draft from 1770 already contains major aspects of the later book.

These are the two basic points: sculpture and painting are essentially different forms of art; and these two arts pertain to two different senses: painting to the visual sense, sculpture to *Gefühl* (touch). *Gefühl* is a fundamental sense that allows the very young child to explore the world. It is the sense that reveals the third dimension, the bodily form. Seeing relates only to surfaces, that is, to two dimensions. Once one accepts these premises, a number of implications become apparent. The mixture of painting and sculpture should be rejected; neither should paintings be made into relief, nor does sculpture need to be decorative. For Herder, antique Greek art is the true, perhaps the only, model for sculpture. In this respect Herder remains a follower of Winckelmann. We have to bear in mind that the style of paintings that was familiar to Herder was Baroque and Rococo art of the seventeenth and eighteenth centuries, with the addition of some bourgeois realism of the later eighteenth century. Herder therefore has some justification to consider the art of painting an art of illusion, and he can say, "Sculpture is *truth,* painting *dream;* the former entirely *representation,* the latter narrative *magic,* what a difference!" (*SW,* 8:17). The truth of sculpture consists in the representation of the human body. Statues can only be truly called sculpture if they reveal the body. Statues hiding the body may have their function in religion or may be allegorical representations of concepts, but they do not properly belong to the plastic arts. Few periods of human history were capable of producing true sculpture, above all ancient Greece. Painting, by contrast, is possible at any time. It can cover and hide, where sculpture has to reveal. Sculpture is naked and natural, and thus innocent. Painting may be much more evocative than sculpture. Here is a Protestant clergyman exalting virtuous nakedness over seductive clothing. Herder also equates the beautiful body with the healthy body. He describes the beautiful body in many details and deplores, like Winckelmann before him, that the customs of the time forbid him to be more specific. Nature as portrayed by the Greeks is beautiful nature, not crude nature. Herder rejects repulsiveness in the visual arts, especially in sculpture, but he accepts the ugliness of centaurs and similar creatures of the mythological imagination. He values truth and vitality over softness and harmony. He insists on the dynamic moment essential for sculpture. The incipient moments of actions give life to statues. Statues have to be, as it were, pregnant with action. Allegories are essentially static and cannot be true art.

Although at first sight Herder seems to support classicism in sculpture, his true values are vitality, dynamics, truth, and motion. No academic art could meet his demands. Herder opposes decorative plastic art and conventions as well as prudish prejudices. He asks the painters to create a magic new world. While insisting on beauty, his basic premises offer painters new freedom to shape their inner visions. Certainly, Herder's sympathy lies with the simplicity, nakedness, and truth of sculpture; he exalts the sense of touch over vision. He feels close to elementary human emotions and experiences; sculpture embodies something of the early human beings. Herder defends the historic justification of heroic art in the form of colossal statues. Sculpture is capable of portraying the sublime instead of the merely beautiful, revealing greatness rather than intimacy. He attacks moral censorship in the arts and the taboo of the naked body through its association with sin. Nakedness is innocence, health; decadence would rather be found in suggestive paintings.

Herder's book not only calls for a reorientation in the arts; it also fits into the general reform movement for naturalness against the artificiality of rococo court life. Herder liked hiking in nature; he refused to wear wigs; he preferred country cooking and simple pleasures. Goethe was a great champion of ice skating. The idea of a healthy mind in a healthy body was gaining ground. The imitation of the Greeks implied the recognition of the significance of the healthy as well as the beautiful body. Herder was keenly interested in physiognomics, and collaborated, like Goethe, in Lavater's monumental undertaking. Although he disclaimed any physiognomic intent in the *Plastic Arts,* he still subscribed to the belief that the body reveals the soul, and that sculpture provides significant examples of male and female beauty and greatness.

Inevitably Herder slips in a survey of the history of art, sculpture in particular, to demonstrate why true sculpture had been impossible in most cultures and ages. In his approach, he shies away from too much theorizing and instead uses psychological experiments, like those with blind people. Aesthetics means sense-related experience. He relates the arts to everyday experiences, and to sensualism in general. He would certainly not have condoned the separation of art objects and performances from the rest of life—for example, museums, libraries, concerts—because art is there to influence the daily life of people through sensual experience.

How to Become a Minister

Training and guiding young ministers was an urgent need for the church of Sachsen-Weimar. Herder hoped to establish a seminar for young theologians. In this context, he wrote his *Briefe, das Studium der Theologie betreffend* (Letters concerning the study of theology) in four parts, published in 1780 and 1781. Their success made a revised edition necessary (1785 and 1786). The Lutheran church was then trying to come to grips with the onslaught of Enlightenment criticism. In particular, it had been challenged by the *Fragments* of the radical Bible criticism of Herman Samuel Reimarus (1694–1768) published by Lessing in the seventies, and the infamous dispute between Lessing and Johann Melchoir Goeze (1717–86), the pugnacious orthodox minister from Hamburg, caused by it. While Herder did not enter this controversy, he sided with Lessing and urged him to publish Reimarus's entire work. He was enthusiastic about *Nathan der Weise* and *The Education of Mankind,* Lessing's last works occasioned by this feud, and saddened by Lessing's untimely death early in 1781, at a time when Lessing and Herder began to be closer.[5] He wrote a moving eulogy for Lessing and continued to discuss problems raised in Lessing's late writings.[6] The *Letters* signal a break with the zealous spirit of Lavater and an urban approach to religion and the ministry, such as is typical for the following works, *The Spirit of Hebrew Poetry,* the *Ideas,* and *God.*

The inner unity of the first two parts of the *Letters,* which deal directly with the biblical text, is evident. The first part serves as a guide to the reading of the Old Testament, the second to that of the New Testament. Herder still elaborates on the *Oldest Document.* The emphasis, however, is different. The Bible, he now declares, is a human document, "and the best reading of this divine book is *human"* (*SW,* 10:7). In other words, the Bible is the poetic and historical account of the beginnings of humanity. Robert Lowth, whose work on the poetic beauties of the Bible Herder respects, made one fundamental error: he had the wrong concept of poetry by wanting to rehabilitate Hebrew poetry in terms of eighteenth-century ideas. But to Herder its very primitivism was essential, as it was the expression of early man, and divinely inspired. The Bible stories are *Geschichte* (history) but not fables or allegories. The story of Genesis is not figuratively true but historical. It is told, however, in childlike simplicity and describes the father-child relationship of God and man. This is the basis for understanding the events and symbols of Genesis. Moreover, the Genesis story was incorporated into a history of Israel, as told by Moses, but certainly based on earlier documents, written or oral. The early parts of the Bible still show the character of simple and short poetic statements typical of ancient human documents. There is more and deeper truth in these simple stories than in subsequent elaborate poetry and prose.

Between the first and the second edition of the *Letters, Vom Geist der Ebräischen Poesie* (The spirit of Hebrew poetry), 1782–83, had appeared, which dealt with the poetic elements of the Old Testament. Still, even the second edition of the *Letters* devotes again much space to the demonstration of the poetic nature of the sacred book of the Jews. Herder did not mince words. The Song of Songs, as he had already stated in his *Lieder der Liebe* (Songs of love, 1778), was a collection of love songs with a literal meaning. The Bible text grew out of historical conditions that were very different from the prudish eighteenth century.

Herder's grand design was to prove or to make plausible that there was a plan in God's creation, and that this plan had to proceed from modest and inconspicuous beginnings through many vicissitudes to an anticipated glorious end. In this developmental plan, the fall of man was necessary, even beneficial. The steps of the development of the human race were economic, necessary, and will prove to be good. As humanity began from one source, it will be reunited in the end. Herder tries to harmonize laws of natural development with God's education of mankind that began with their creation: humanity stands under the law of learning and education.

In his commentary on the New Testament, where Herder faced an especially critical and suspicious readership, he pleaded, first of all, for the credibility of the chroniclers who wrote the four gospels and the epistles. Matthew, Mark, and Luke simply wrote down what they knew about Jesus and considered significant for the faithful to know. In contrast to St. John, they did not intend to teach but told their stories without an ulterior design. Much of what they had to say went against the beliefs of the age and Jewish traditions, and this enhances their credibility. Christianity is a universal religion starting from humble and obscure beginnings, which is in keeping with Herder's general view of history. If God sent his son to this earth to redeem humanity, he had to make him thoroughly human and have him live through the full range of human experiences. Thus there is no contradiction between the very human personality of Jesus and the message of the gospels. It could be misleading to read Herder's exegesis in a secularized manner. He is rather traditional in opposing deism on more orthodox grounds than he himself may have thought. Interestingly, for Herder, as for Lessing's Nathan, it is the unbroken tradition that guarantees the truth of the gospels and the historicity of the Christian religion.

The tradition is one of active Christian life, not one of dogma, which Herder rejects as inessential. Christianity proves itself through the lives and examples of true Christians. It is the religion of active love and is based on God's love for men, and men's love for each other.

The miracles, so prominent in the discussion of the *Fragments*, do not bother Herder. Everything hinges on the credibility of the evangelists. Their accounts are those of inspired writers, not scientists. Still, Herder prefers commonsense explanations wherever possible, insisting on the different mentality of the people at the time of Jesus Christ.

In the third and fourth parts of the *Letters*, Herder turns to the practical problems of the ministry. He denies contradictions between revelation and reason, Bible and nature, common sense and religion. He moves along the same lines of argumentation as Lessing's *Education of Mankind* and reformulates its basic thesis that revelation is the education of the human race (*SW*, 10:286). It is essential to maintain the tradition through the living, spoken word, which cannot be replaced by its poor substitute, writing. Consequently, Herder devotes much of the two last parts to problems of preaching and teaching. The minister is, first of all, a preacher who communicates the message of religion. He has to avoid unnecessary subtleties and convey his essential message in a lively manner, without undue ornamentation. Sacred poetry and its rendering of truth may inspire him; and the Book of Job, like some other parts of the Bible, could be regarded as the highest form of didactic poetry (11:65).

In Herder's view, the young student of theology should not read too much. Indiscriminate reading is one of the curses of the present age; it is better to read fewer books, but in greater depth. One should form one's convictions before wading through the maze of diverging opinions typical of contemporary discussions. This does not mean that one should have a closed mind and become dogmatic; it only says that one should understand essential points of human existence before being exposed to all those confusing opinions. Rousseau's Émile was to be brought up outside of society before confronting it. Certainly, for Herder, there are important books, like those of Shaftesbury, Rousseau, and Montesquieu, and there are books that could be dangerous for an unprepared young mind, like those of Voltaire and Lamettrie. As far as the Bible is concerned, any philological explanations and commentaries are welcome, whereas critical treatises on the Bible should wait for later. While opposing censorship and the suppression of books by government and churches, Herder increasingly saw the need for a pedagogical approach to the proper reading of young theologians. This view was confirmed by the visits of the young Swiss student of theology Georg Müller, brother of the historian Johannes von Müller, whose studies in Göttingen had led him into a severe crisis. Herder's personal influence helped to solve the crisis, and Müller remained a loyal friend of the family, proving his devotion by his selfless work on the edition of Herder's works after his death. Herder had students like Müller in mind when he wrote the *Letters* and their sequel, *The Spirit of Hebrew Poetry*. The work grew out of a potential fifth part of the *Letters*, called "Letters to Theophron." One of the major reasons for this emphasis on the poetic and historical qualities was the widespread practice, especially by pietists and other fundamentalists, to use isolated Bible quotations for their dogmatic purposes.

The Spirit of Hebrew Poetry was designed for the "amateurs of this poetry and the oldest history of the human race." It is not a book for theologians and about theology. Herder addresses a message similar to that of the *Letters* to a general audience that knows most of the Bible by heart but rarely appreciates it. Herder's spokesman in the dialogue part of the book, Eutyphron, derives pleasure from reading this ancient poetry; but this is not really Herder's main point. Hebrew poetry is national poetry, representing the feelings and aspirations of an entire people, and it is sacred poetry revealing truth. Herder's favorite books are evident: Genesis, the Song of Songs, Job, and everything relating to David, as well as most of the Psalms. In an urbane and soft-spoken dialogue, Eutyphron and Alciphron go once more over the ground of the *Oldest Document,* with Alciphron mentioning the objections against it (*SW,* 11:246). Eutyphron, however, defends the essential truth of the central metaphor that dawn is creation. Herder provides samples of poetry in his own translation and helps the reader to appreciate them. His larger designs are kept in the background. He follows the historical sequence and thus offers a cultural history of the people of Israel, its rise and decline. The emphasis, however, is on the Hebrew language and poetic devices. Especially in the second part, where the dialogue form is abandoned, a systematic survey of different poetic genres, particularly the Psalms, is given. The expertise of the historian, the theologian, and the literary critic are in evidence. Poetry from the Bible is folk art. Folk songs are not merely those whose author had remained anonymous and hailed from the lower classes. For Herder, folk song expressed the spirit of the people and was representative of collective feelings, no matter who the creator was, king or peasant, an unknown poet or a great writer. Folk songs voiced common concerns in war and peace, work and celebration; they expressed love, joy, sadness, parting and meeting, life and death. They sang about nature and God. In order to render the situations of Hebrew poetry plausible, Herder personalized and individualized the poems as much as possible, in contrast to the depersonalized views of folk art in the nineteenth century. It is not an accident that Herder's interest in folk songs of all peoples runs parallel to his view of the Bible. Both serve one purpose and are part of his overall view of the history of mankind.

The Great Work

Herder did not want to reissue *Another Philosophy,* after the first edition had been exhausted. He still had the dreams of the *Diary* present in his mind, but after going through the usual stages from high hopes and expectations to growing self-doubts, he wrote a work that he considered preliminary, and which he modestly called *Ideen zur Philosophie der Geschichte der Menschheit* (Ideas for a philosophy of the history of Humankind). Even in this more modest scope, the work remained unfinished, and the fifth part was never written. It would have taken the story to the present age; but some of its contents were scattered among Herder's later collections, especially the *Letters for the Advancement of Humanity*. Beyond all personal and political reasons for the abandonment of the project, there was an irreconcilable contradiction between Herder's view of the history of the human race and his attitude toward his own age.

The first parts of the *Ideas,* however, were written at a time when Herder had reason to be fairly satisfied. In 1783 the friendship with Goethe had been renewed and seemed closer than ever. Herder, the writer, was no longer the lone voice of the Bückeburg days, but representative of the growing class of the *Gebildeten,* the progressive educated group from both nobility and middle class. The new national *Bildung,* including educational ideals, ethics of self-responsibility, stress on respect for human rights and individual feelings, and a new religious attitude, depended largely on the writings of Lessing, Wieland, Goethe, Schiller, and certainly Herder, who exemplified true humanistic *Bildung* in a new idiom—the new German language that became the common bond of the people before any political sense of unity. The educated public of a subsequent age may have taken Herder's contributions for granted, but it valued his works of the eighties, all the more so since he did not yet stand in the shadow of Goethe. Goethe was still the author of *Werther;* his more mature works did not appear until the last years of the decade. It was the time when Herder could feel most appreciated and most in harmony with his potential audience.

The concept of universal history was common to the later eighteenth century. Herder had been in controversy on that subject with August Ludwig von Schlözer (1735–1809), a professor at Göttingen. He knew of course Voltaire, Hume, and Gibbon. Isaak Iselin (1728–82) had published in 1764 a popular *Geschichte der Menschheit* (History of Mankind), largely directed against Rousseau. Herder's relationship with and knowledge of Giovanni Battista Vico (1668–1744) is still in doubt, as there is little direct documentation.[7] Justus Möser had original thoughts on this matter, and Kant was also developing his theory of the history of mankind. The eighteenth century found it imperative to provide a universal historical ori-

entation. Historians had to write the history of mankind. The rise
and fall of nations and cultures were to be seen in a universal
framework.

Herder's contribution to the philosophy of history went beyond
the organicist concept and the relative stress on individual cultures
that are customarily attributed to him. He situated the planet Earth
within the universe and saw human life as part of organic life on
this earth. He posited universal laws governing all life. History is
thus a natural development; however, nature and history are also
realizations of a divine plan of creation. Herder's interpretation of
nature and history, especially human history, is religiously motivated, but he was very careful not to ascribe religious reasons and
meanings to individual phenomena and developments. He is suspicious of "systems." His religious humanism is based on the conviction of *Ganzheit* (totality), which would preclude an arbitrary
separation of the realm of nature and the realm of freedom. The
creation is indivisible.

Herder was convinced that empirical data would confirm his ideas,
so he tried to keep up with the advances in the life sciences. He
encouraged Goethe's scientific research and was the recipient of the
latter's jubilant letter announcing the discovery of the intermaxillary
bone, the missing link between human beings and the animal world.
Goethe and Herder believed in the chain of beings, and their Dar-
winism before Darwin should be seen with a grain of salt.[8] Herder
in particular could not conceive of the human being as developing
from animals. In his view, humans were essentially different even
from the nearest animals. A biological evolution from animals to
the human species was outside of his thinking, which was still
influenced by the idea of divine creation. This is what he meant
when he apologized in his preface for using the word *nature* in a
personified sense. "Nature is not an independent being, *but God is
everything in His Works*" (*SW*, 13:9–10). Since he addressed a scientific age, Herder shied away from invoking God's name too much.
God is *Allerhalter, pantokrator*, sustaining life in the universe; but
then, He cannot be separated from nature and is not extramundane.
While Herder was writing the first part of the *Ideas*, the Spinoza
debate had begun. He heard to his joy about Lessing's insistence
on *hen kai pan*, and expressed his convictions in a long letter to
Friedrich Heinrich Jacobi of 6 February 1784 (*Br*, 5:27–29).

The first part of the *Ideas* describes the earth within the cosmos and life on earth with reference to the human race. The second part explains the nature of humanity in general terms, whereas the third and fourth parts present Herder's historical and anthropological survey of human cultures. The survey breaks off with the transition from the Middle Ages to the modern period, which was to be treated in a fifth part.

According to Herder, the earth is a star among stars; in fact, it is the "middle" planet in the planetary system. The habitat of the human being is between the extremes, just as the human being is a creature of the middle. This human habitat has had a long history. The present extent and shape of mountains and seas is the result of many "revolutions" (*SW*, 13:21), that is, cyclical changes. Even if such revolutions may appear chaotic and cruel for an individual at a particular point in time, they are in accordance with the laws of nature. Nature offers the greatest possible variety on the basis of an underlying unity and simplicity (13:22). Already anorganic nature shows specific forms and laws of formation; organic nature even more so. Herder demonstrates development and distribution of minerals and their significance for organic life. He is sympathetic to plant life, his major source for imagery besides astronomy, mindful "that human life, insofar it is vegetation, has also the fate of the plants" (13:52). Development from seeds was controversial at the time. The theory of preformation, which assumed a tiny model of the future plant in the seed or germ, was being debated and contested. Herder's main interest was the principle of entelechia. By this he understood that every being is endowed with vital forces that work for the realization of its unique potential. It is the fate of living beings that the realization of their fullest form is the beginning of the end, the first step toward death. Plants demonstrate the conservation of the species in procreation (13:54). They adapt themselves to different climates and soils and respond to the passing of the days and seasons.

As far as the animal kingdom is concerned, nature wanted to create the largest number and greatest variety of living beings in the smallest possible space (13:61). This leads to close interaction and mutual interdependence of the various parts of the environment. In this natural environment, man is a *Mittelgeschöpf*, a "medial" creature (*SW*, 13:65) among the animals. Herder assumes a prototype *(Hauptform)* of animals that he assumes to be similar to the human being. Whereas Goethe was looking for basic elements to

establish his *Urpflanze* and *Urtier,* Herder moved backward from
the human being. He surmised that the closer the animals are to
the humans, the more similarities they have with them (13:67).
Herder is not far from instituting comparative anatomy. However,
he remains anthropocentric. What he really wants to prove is that
the human being combines the best features of the various animal
species (13:68). Still, he pays close attention to similarities of all
kinds of life on earth and the laws of organic nature. He never
departs from this principle: "Where there is effect, there must be
a force; where there is new life, there must be a principle of the
new life" (13:86). This vital principle inheres in the driving forces,
not in the seeds themselves.

Describing the structure of the various kinds of animals, Herder
is leading to the final comparison with man: the uniqueness of
human beings is proved by their upright posture (*SW,* 13:110).
This upright posture and walk is not found among animals but is
specifically human (13:112). Herder specifies this distinction in his
comparison of the human species with the orangutan in the first
section of the fourth book. The upright position brought about a
different form of the head that is characterized by a high forehead
and corresponding differences in the brain. This leads to the specifically human proportions and to human beauty. The erect posture
provides for a unique perspective on the world. The vertical axis
becomes crucial: man looks upward. The human being "is what he
is supposed to be (and all parts participate in this), a tree striving
upward, crowned with the most beautiful crown of a *finer formation
of thoughts"* (13:131). Because of this vertical (as against a horizontal)
organization, the human being is made for finer perceptions, for
language, and for the arts. The upright gait makes the human being
into a *Kunstgeschöpf* (13:137) who produces artifices. In its fight for
survival, the human being finds and makes weapons for defense. By
nature, however, human beings have neither teeth nor claws but
are peaceful (13:138). They are not naturally aggressive. The link
between language and reason is vital for the beginning and development of the human race. However, the human race should not
divorce itself from other living species. As the embryo goes through
all the developmental stages of living creatures on earth (13:142),
the plant and animal stages inhere in the human being, except that
there they are controlled by reason. Man is born only with a potential
for reason, which has to be acquired through learning. This potential

implies a potential for freedom, which sets the human beings apart from the animals: "The human being is the first freed creature of creation; it stands upright" (13:146). Man's hands are free, he choses between alternatives. But even though freedom makes misuse possible, this very misuse proves the humanity of humans. Without this freedom, social life could not be organized, nor could marriage, government, the striving for truth, or happiness. *Selbstbestimmung* (self-determination) is the fundamental human trait (13:149).

With the upright position and freedom comes the adaptability of human beings to different climates. Nature made humans masters of the earth. The human being is destined for *Humanität,* which makes humans different from other living creatures. Herder tried many times to define this elusive but central term of his later years. He found the traits of self-preservation and communication with others (*SW,* 13:155), exemplified by such features as the sex drive. While humans share such characteristics with animals, they fulfill them in their own ways. Sex in humans is elevated to love, and human beings are sympathetic to others beyond the capabilities of animals. From this basic sympathy, Herder derives the ideas of justice and truth. Men understand the basic rule not to do to others what they do not want done to themselves (13:160). Religion is the highest form of *Humanität* (13:161) and the human being is formed for the hope of immortality (13:165–66).

In recapitulating in the fifth book the points made in the first four, Herder stresses the chain of ascending forms and forces in nature. The more highly organized a living being is, the more elements from lower beings are contained in it. Each natural force has an organ, but one should not confuse such organs with the natural forces working through them. Forces may be present before they enter into physical organs, and may continue to exist after the death of that organism. Herder admits that he has problems defining in scientific terms these life-giving forces (*SW,* 13:175–76), and it thus appears more like a metaphysical principle to ensure immortality. *Fortschreitung* (progress) comes through the connection of forces and forms (13:177). Such progress is present in the ascending chain of organisms, but also in the history of human consciousness. Humans are organized in a system of *geistige* (spiritual) forces. If the goal of life is *Humanität,* very little of it is realized in one individual human life. Thus this life is a *Vorübung* (preparation). It is the bud for a future bloom and fruit—to use Herder's own metaphors.

Herder's "probable" hypothesis (13:194) would be, consequently, that the present state of mankind is a link between two worlds: the animal world and the world of *gottähnliche Humanität* (13:191). Since everything in nature is connected and shows gradual development, how can the dualistic nature of man and the contradictions in the human condition be otherwise explained?

Herder's model situates the human race within the framework of nature, within the universe and on this planet. Herder is fighting on two fronts: he wants to replace the old metaphysical world view with a philosophy that takes into account the advances of the sciences. On the other hand, he clearly combats rationalistic science and psychology. He denies the adequacy of mechanistic explanations of nature, and he opposes the most consistent system of social psychology of the rationalists, that of Helvetius. Whereas Helvetius saw self-interest of individuals and groups as the decisive force in the organization of the human race, Herder bases human self-preservation not on egotism but on sympathy and love, on caring for each other. He adheres to the eighteenth-century view of the double nature of man as a mixture of angel and beast, as Haller's famous formula had it. He could not bear to reduce the human race to mere animals; nor would he deny their animal nature. Out of the contradictions of human nature he discerned a better future, both on this earth and elsewhere, although he was extremely cautious in the formulation of his utopian expectation, especially when compared to Lessing, Fichte, and the romanticists.

In the second part, Herder provides the fundamentals for the social organization of the human race. He follows Montesquieu in stressing the influence of the climate. "Climate" has a wide meaning for Herder. In an ethnological sketch, he surveys peoples near the North Pole, in Asia, Africa, and the Americas, and in the middle regions of the earth, and deduces their physical culture, customs, and mentality from their physical environment. While he tries to do justice to each region, he always adheres to aesthetic criteria in evaluating culture. He is obviously most interested in *schöngebildete* (beautifully formed) peoples (*SW*, 13:221). The first people of this kind that he deals with in section 3 of book 6 is the people of India, specifically Kashmir (13:221). Kashmir, Herder says here and later, may have been Paradise—the Garden of Eden—and the first habitat of human beings.[9] Here he replaces China—which had been considered by the earlier Enlightenment as the mother country of civilization.[10] Herder's image of Kashmir and India is the prelude to the romantic image of India and the search for salvation in that culture.

Cultures and races differ greatly, but they share common elements, just as no two leaves are alike though they are leaves of one tree (*SW*, 13:252). The course of human life is that of progressive metamorphosis (13:253–54), of constant change. Men come in many shapes and forms, but are still human beings. In contrast to all animals, including the apes, there is only one human race with one common ideal and one set of characteristics. Herder is hesitant about making final determinations. He declines to give a verdict on the impact of the environment on human beings. Perhaps, he says, the colonization of other continents and climates by Europeans may yield an answer of how much people change in a different climate. Herder fears negative consequences from a radical change of the environment. The colonists cannot and should not change their new environments into another Europe (13:286–87); nature might avenge crimes committed against her (13:289). It seems wiser to adapt oneself to a new climate and aim for a gradual change. Herder abhorred the exploitation of the other continents by Europeans and never condoned slavery. He felt it was wrong to remake the earth in one's own image. Man is not Prometheus, but a mortal creature, an organism composed of the elements of nature, and therefore ready to return to nature. A technological civilization would thus not constitute progress, but the degradation of life into a machine.

Behind the discussion of the diversity of cultures lurks another problem: the question of a common origin of the human race. While Herder favored this concept, he did not insist on proof.

As Herder sees it, the five human senses and their proper usage work in interaction with the environment. Imagination depends on climate and environment. Also, practical skills and understanding are generated by necessity and specific conditions. The perceptions and drives of people must be in harmony with their conditions: people are governed by habits and opinions arising from their living conditions. Herder cited as an example the relationship of men and women. He tries to show why women introduced a sense of cleanliness, tolerance, delicacy, beauty, and finer emotions, such as the love of a mother for her child, into society, and why in most civilizations the men subjugated the women. He makes extensive use of accounts of travels in other continents and always searches in so-called primitive peoples for forms of social organization that can no longer be found in advanced cultures.

Happiness is crucial for any eighteenth-century philosopher. Its very name, *Glückseligkeit,* indicates, as Herder says, that the human being is a child of fortune *(Glück)* and subject to the changes of fortune *(SW,* 13:333). Happiness can only be individual, never collective. There is a built-in measure in things and beings. No human happiness can be boundless; it is limited by natural laws and boundaries. Individuals are not made for the state. The machinelike state must make individuals unhappy in order to achieve its aims, and the bigger it is, the less regard it has for the individual. Providence wanted the human race to be happy; but the organization of human society as a state creates unhappiness. Therefore, states cannot be the rightful purpose of humanity, they are aberrations.

In book 9, Herder investigates the principles and forms of social organization. Man is not a *Selbstgebohrner,* not "self-born" *(SW,* 13:344). He depends on others for physical existence and education. The history of mankind is a chain of social and educational traditions. Lessing's phrase "education of mankind" can only be applied to the individual, Herder says. Man grows through education, and the human race is a chain of such individuals. However, it is best to avoid abstractions such as are constituted by terms like "the human race." Parents and teachers educate children in a concrete environment, and families form the nucleus of clans and tribes and thus of peoples. The history of mankind is governed by tradition and organic forces (13:347). It does not matter whether one calls this education of a child *Kultur* or *Aufklärung* (culture or enlightenment) (13:348); it is still this chain of *Bildung* which is the real history of humanity and without which the past would only be a horrible chaos of destruction and ugliness.

The foremost means and medium for the education and *Bildung* of human beings is language. A comparative analysis and history of languages would yield the most intimate insights into cultures and their development. However, let us be mindful of the character of this instrument. We do not express things, but names; we find characteristic traits of things which are words *(SW,* 13:358). Thus we cannot express pure perceptions; we do not perceive things in themselves. However, pure speculation is not cognition—which comes through the verbal expression by reason of sense data. Language is limited to the field of experience, and linguistic expression, if meaningful, is close to practical concerns. For Herder, the link between reason and language is essential, as is the historical and cultural interpretation of linguistic structures, as well as the distrust of purely intellectual systems. The more "advanced" a civilization is the more it can avail itself of inventions, art, and science, and derive power from them. However, a civilization that has inherited such inventions and makes use of them should not attribute to itself the creative powers to make them. This criticism is directed mainly against modern Europeans, who subjugate the rest of the world through such power. For Herder there is a basic difference between the satisfaction of genuine needs and technological power beyond real needs. He makes this evident in section 4 where he deals with the different forms of government. Herder had trouble writing and rewriting this section in a form that would be palatable to the contemporary audience, represented by Goethe, as he told Hamann (April 1785; *Br,* 5:121). He still insisted on the distinction between natural government, formed on a voluntary basis because of need, and despotic government generated by war and conquest. The European conquest, for example, destroyed the natural societies of the other continents (*SW,* 13:451). Kant had just stated in his *Idee zu einer allgemeinen Geschichte in welt-bürgerlicher Absicht* (Idea for a General History with a Cosmopolitan Intent) of 1784 that the human being was an animal that needed a master. On the contrary, Herder replies, a human being who needs a master is an animal; when he becomes a real human being, he does not need a master (13:383). Human beings need each other: man needs woman, the child needs parents, the sick person needs a doctor, people in dispute need a judge, a group needs a leader. However, only those human beings who are considered weak and not yet adult or self-reliant need a despotic master. The natural function of a state is to provide mutual help and security. Hereditary rule is inherently bad. Why should the son of a great leader or judge follow in his father's footsteps? As he had said in the *Diary,* Herder would like to replace Montesquieu's work by a true history of governments (13:386–87). The oldest and holiest tradition on earth is religion. Although priests have often misused their powers, it would be wrong to drive out religion. Religion was the first and fundamental element of human culture and tradition (13:390); it should be reformed and strengthened and not abolished.

In book 10, Herder provides a transition from his discussion of

principles to his survey of human history. He discusses the origin
of the human race and covers much of the same ground as in the
Oldest Document. This tenth book, in the middle of the work, may
indeed have a pivotal position. For Herder, the question of the
origin of the human race is of prime importance. Since the sources
lead to an origin in Asia, Herder examines Asian traditions about
the creation of the earth and the origin of mankind. These relate
that the earth was first empty and chaotic and covered by a dark
sea. Then there was light. The first human beings lived in a garden
in Western Asia, where a great river originated, which was subsequently divided into four main rivers (13:431). This must have
been, according to Herder, among the mountains of northern India,
probably in Kashmir. Since so little was known about the most
ancient Indian traditions, Herder followed the account in Genesis.

Having thus provided the basis for a chronological history, Herder
surveys the ancient world in part 3 and the Middle Ages in part 4.
His overview of ancient culture goes from east to west, beginning
with China. Still adhering to the developmental pattern of childhood, youth, adult, and old age, Herder evaluates different cultures
according to their developmental stages. He considers that Far Eastern cultures, including China, were stopped at an early stage and
have stagnated ever since. He also criticizes the Indian social system,
believing that the Brahmins held back the organic growth of Indian
culture. Considering Herder's enthusiasm for Hebrew poetry, it is
also surprising that he views the history of the people of Israel with
some critical distance. The uncertainty of the borders, too many
political changes and disruptions, and the despotism of the native
kings prevented the people of Israel from developing their potential.
Herder praises the greatness of the religious books of the Hebrews
but deplores their narrow-minded application. Christianity, he argues, is a logical outcome of the Jewish culture in decay. While he
has rather harsh words for the role of the Jews among the peoples
in later ages, he attributes their faults more to their condition than
to their character: "Briefly, it is a people whose education was spoiled
because it never reached the maturity of political culture on its own
soil, and thus the true feeling of honor and freedom" (*SW,* 14:67).
The history of Asia teaches us that the organization of states, societies, and religions can be as much a hindrance for the development
of a culture as it is its necessary support system. While religious
and political systems reflect the need of the peoples of the time

when they are instituted, the same peoples can outgrow them, and thus those systems can be stifling. Both empty ceremonies in religions and political despotism that keeps the subjects in a childlike state are to be rejected.

Herder finds many reasons to describe ancient Greece with particular sympathy. Greece, for him, was the one culture permitted to grow through all life stages and thus to develop its fullest potential. Islands and peninsulas, Herder observes, have produced freer and more variegated forms of culture than the great land masses. Greece was favored by its geographical shape as well as by its climate and location. Herder explains how the arts rose to such perfection. Both political constitutions and sports, and especially religion, favored the expression of a *Gemeingeist* (communal spirit) (*SW*, 14:111) in artistic form. Whereas the variety of so many Greek states was initially good for freedom and culture, the internal strife, combined with the wealth and luxury after the Persian wars, became one of the causes of their downfall. Greece still exemplifies the principle: "What can happen in the realm of humanity within the bounds of given national, historical, and local conditions, will happen in reality, and Greece offers the richest and most beautiful proofs of this" (14:144). Culture is the flower of a people's existence, but the flower also indicates its mortality (14:147). Greece also proves another Herderian theorem: the health and duration of a state does not depend on a few outstanding achievements, but on the balance of its vital forces. The lower the center of gravity in culture, the more solid is the structure (14:149). A culture built on the masses of the lower classes will be durable, while mere aristocratic cultures are delicate and transitory phenomena.

Rome invokes ambivalent feelings in Herder, as book 14 makes evident. Rome destroyed other ancient cultures, including Greece, Carthage, and Israel. However, the Latin tongue is the medium through which the remnants of the ancient cultures are preserved. The ruins of Rome offer perspectives beyond Rome itself. Although modern life has little in common with ancient Rome, Latin is still the medium for the tradition of Western culture.

The Romans were a warlike people, which is proved by the Roman constitution. This in turn gave rise to the celebrated Roman virtue. Thus virtue and the political constitution came to an end at the same time (*SW*, 165). The universal principle of *Wiedervergeltung* or *nemesis* is particularly evident in the case of Rome (14:177). History tends toward a balance, and crimes against other peoples will always find their revenge. Herder also goes into specific reasons for the fall of Rome: the antagonisms in its original constitution between different social partners; the contradiction between city state and world power; slavery and luxury; but above all, the *Kriegsgeist* (warlike spirit) (14:185) that will finally judge and destroy itself. He acknowledges Roman greatness and regrets that so much of Roman literature and historiography is lost.

The last book of each part draws general conclusions from the material surveyed. This is particularly obvious for book 15, which contrasts a pessimistic and an optimistic view of history. Herder felt that he had to counter the many pessimistic commentaries on the fall of Rome, notably by Gibbon. His decisive argument, however, exceeds empirical historiography: "If there is a God in nature, he is also in history; for the human being, too, is part of the creation and must follow laws, even in his wildest deviations and passions, that are no less beautiful and excellent than those according to which all celestial and terrestrial bodies move" (*SW*, 14:207). Human nature is destined for *Humanität*, and God has given the human race freedom to reach this destiny. Freedom is freedom to err and also to destroy. But the destructive forces in nature and history are weaker than the forces of conservation. Destruction itself is a means for the higher development of the whole (14:213). While, in his view, the history of mankind is too short to yield general laws, Herder still believes in the function of destruction for betterment and perfection. Inventions have been beneficial on the whole; and progress is undeniable even in the art of government, the most difficult of all arts.

Herder, believing in *nemesis* as an ultimate law of justice in history, sees an increase in *Billigkeit* (reason and justice) to ensure the welfare of the human race. While the developmental model still holds true and no optimal state can ever last, since forces and systems are in constant flux, Herder believes in a fundamental goodness in the fate of human beings (*SW*, 14:244). The fifteenth book, published in 1787, two years before the French Revolution, eloquently summarizes Herder's faith in God, nature, and history, and in the ultimate victory of the principle of *Humanität*.

The fourth part of the book did not appear until 1791. Herder was excited by the political events and progressed with increasing difficulty. Surprisingly, there is no genuine summary at the end of this last part. The twentieth book describes the transition from the Middle Ages to the modern era and the roots of the modern spirit in medieval times. The author obviously left his final comment on Europe for his projected last part.

Herder concentrated on two major concerns: the evaluation of the historical role of Christianity, and the history of the Germanic peoples, that is, the roots of his own culture. Herder was no advocate of Germanic supremacy; he repeats his unequivocal condemnation of the cruelties of the Order of Teutonic Knights and expresses his sympathy for the suffering Slavic peoples, such as the Latvians and the now extinct Prussians. For him, the Germanic peoples developed heroic virtues, since they were strong and eager for conquests, but they neglected peaceful endeavors, such as agriculture. They had to import higher culture into Northern Europe and would not have risen to higher levels by their own forces (*SW*, 14:289). Yet, it was because of their wars that a common spirit and something of a melting pot had developed in Europe.

In book 17, devoted to the rise of Christianity, Herder found one more opportunity to praise Jesus Christ and his religion, from which, in his view, the most genuine *Humanität* emanated. Jesus, the *Menschensohn*, is the very essence of humanity. Christianity was to be a *Bund* (alliance) based on friendship and brotherly love and governed by elders and teachers. No hierarchy and only a minimum of ceremonies were intended: the two sacraments of Baptism and Communion and the confession of faith in the Father, Son, and Holy Spirit. The religion of Jesus, who was opposed to too much ritual, differed fundamentally from that of the Christian Churches, and could never have been a state religion. Due to the various cultural and historical conditions in the Orient and the Occident, Christianity was fundamentally transformed. It became the Byzantine state religion which Herder abhors (*SW*, 14:330) and the Roman Catholic hierarchy and worship of graves (14:334). Herder agrees with Gibbon in his treatment of the early churches. He tried hard to be fair, but still saw few signs of an advancement of humanity.

The rapid conquest of many European countries by the Germanic peoples and the early demise of their states are explained by the fact that a small war-loving aristocracy is not sufficient to sustain a society. In addition, the communal property system, the general freedom, and the exaggerated power of the kings caused inner dissensions, even fragmentation. Thus the kings were replaced by dukes who usurped their authority. They were supported by the Roman Catholic clerics, and together they established hierarchies that displaced the original Germanic freedom and equality. One of Herder's lone heroes—an individual in this history without individual heroes—is Charlemagne (*SW*, 14:371–72), to whom he addresses this concluding statement: "Perhaps you will reappear in 1800 and change the machine that began in 800. Until then we want to honor your reliques, legally misuse your laws, and despise your old-fashioned diligence. Great Charles, your empire, which broke up immediately after your death, is your memorial; France, Germany, and Lombardy are its ruins" (14:372). Herder waited for the restoration of Europe and its ancient free constitution. Romanticism was to institute a hero worship of Charlemagne and Barbarossa in the name of German nationalism.

Herder's account of the rule of the Roman Catholic church over Europe could hardly be expected to be favorable. Herder's main objection is the idea of archbishops and bishops governing as secular rulers. He also objected to the control of the church over all social activities. While stressing the civilizing influence of the church in the Middle Ages, Herder finds that it prevented the advancement of the arts and sciences. Medieval art is not Herder's favorite. But beyond questions of taste Herder's opposition is basically political. In his opinion, the church changed the original free spirit of the Germans into a habit of serfdom. The counterforce that inevitably arose originated in the cities; it was the spirit of free enterprise and trade. Contrary to commonly held views, Herder found few good things to say about the Crusades. Certainly they did not cause the subsequent progress of Europe. They were foolish enterprises whose few benefits were accidental and would have come about more easily without them. Herder lovingly describes medieval poetry, as it migrated from the Arabs in Spain to the various European countries. But he is not sympathetic toward chivalry as such. A culture of a caste of warriors (and robbers) can never be truly beneficial. The new progressive spirit was that of useful activities, of competing arts and crafts, of scholarship and science (*SW*, 14:493), opposing knights and monks. The middle class replaced the orders of monks and knights with new types of corporations, with guilds of craftsmen and guilds of scholars called universities. In Herder's time, these corporations had become obsolete, but in the Middle Ages they were necessary for the organization of new inventions, technology, and knowledge. They contributed to the foundation of the *Handelsre-publik,* the republic of traders that was to be the new Europe. Herder's short plan for the five books of part 5 (*SW,* 14:652) shows the emphasis on this line of thought. Book 21 was to describe this emerging commercial and scientific Europe, book 22 the Reformation and book 23 the philosophy of law and science; book 24 was to situate Europe in relation to the other continents, and the concluding book would have discussed *Humanität* as manifested in the various spheres of human activities. Herder would also have discussed the concepts of revolution and perfectibility (14:648–51).

The generally favorable reception of Herder's *magnum opus* was marred by a peculiar discordant note. A new journal in the neighboring town of Jena, the *Allgemeine Literatur-Zeitung,* asked Kant to review the first part of the *Ideas.* When Kant read the book—Hamann had given him a copy—he found much that he disliked. It is still uncertain what motivated him to write such a scathing review. He was certainly justified in pointing out that, for him, Herder's style and approach were unscientific, unclear, and metaphysical. Kant was still fighting for the recognition of his new critical philosophy. He probably felt he had to make a clean break. It would go too far to discuss the merits and demerits of this controversy, which has colored many later judgments of Herder. Herder himself was deeply hurt by such an action from his admired teacher. Here was the beginning of his later anti-Kantian campaign.

Herder's *Ideas* do not seek to present a "system," but they muster an enormous wealth of empirical data to demonstrate certain basic principles and ideas. This demonstration is really what Herder had in mind, although he kept stressing that many of his conclusions were tentative or speculative. Still, he wanted to make it plausible that history, just like nature, obeys general laws that indicate the workings of a benevolent divine spirit. Historical laws are simple and natural. Tradition and natural forms of association are the basis for human society. Cultural history must be understood in analogy with organic life; it follows the sequence of growth, maturity, decay, and transformation. Latent forces strive to become reality. History moves with forces and counterforces, between conservation and destruction; and a law of *nemesis* rules over everything. However, in all "revolutions" a gradual improvement is at work: *Vervollkommnung* (perfectibility) is evident in nature and history.

This rather harmonizing picture of the history of mankind became

somewhat clouded when Herder contemplated his own age. While
he wanted to see the positive signs in this era of crisis, especially
in the French Revolution, he could not overcome his grave doubts.
Moreover, was his audience ready for his message or would part 5
have been so mutilated by censorship and self-censorship that it
would not have been worth printing? In any case, Herder gave up.

Herder's *Ideas* signal a historic transition. While he still adheres
to Enlightenment universalism and the faith in perfectibility, he
stresses the significance for history of the ethnic units and the national character and thus assumes a point of view characteristic of
the beginning of the next century. Herder hated the bureaucratic
state machine and wanted to replace it by natural groups of culturally
united people enjoying peaceful free association. But nationalism
has become the major force for aggression, and the idea of the
organic community has been used to justify the obedience of the
individual to a state, church, cause, or ideology. Herder was not a
forerunner of this type of nationalism; but in his synthesis of Enlightenment universalism and the concept of evolution he not only
accommodated contradictions but also experimented with ideas that
could be distorted and misused. His sometimes hesitant formulations and his metaphorical language enhanced the possibilities of
appropriating isolated quotations for ideological purposes.

There is one timely aspect of the *Ideas* that has until recently been
overlooked. Herder's ethnocentric and evolutionary approach implies
a fundamental critique of the European world view. Mankind is not
identical with Europe, and the European domination of the world
had as many negative as it had positive effects, perhaps even more
of the former. Herder emerges as a champion of small nations and
of the cultures of other continents. Adhering to his own principle
of *nemesis,* he foresees a powerful reaction of the other continents
against violent European colonization.

Jacob Burckhardt has praised Herder for his ingenious combination of specific description and general remarks, insights, and
commmentaries, as well as for his avoidance of a "system" à la
Hegel. Herder did work from specific assumptions, and he presented
a philosophy of history, but since he valued the significance of
empirical evidence, he offered a surprising number of interesting
insights. His *Ideas* also stand out as a monument to the efforts of
the age of Goethe to preserve meaning and direction at a time that
seemed utterly chaotic and destructive.

Spinoza's God

Friedrich Heinrich Jacobi, who was a sincere man struggling to preserve his faith in God, had paid a visit to Lessing in 1780. Lessing, according to Jacobi, had confessed to him that he was convinced of Spinoza's idea of God. This was a revolutionary thought for the time, and Jacobi informed Moses Mendelssohn of this conversation after Lessing had died early in 1781. An epistolary debate ensued between Jacobi and the incredulous Mendelssohn; and these letters were widely circulated. Mendelssohn made every effort to refute Jacobi's report, and Jacobi finally published this exchange in 1785. Mendelssohn died in 1786. Goethe and Herder, both Spinoza devotees, followed these events with excitement and satisfaction Herder was unwilling to leave the last word to either Mendelssohn or Jacobi, since both disagreed with Lessing. Herder was preoccupied with Lessing's later writings, especially with the idea of palingenesis, as can be seen in *Scattered Leaves*. [11] He felt compelled to add his word to the debate on Spinoza [12] and called it *Gott: Einige Gespräche* (God: some conversations). The work appeared in 1787, the same year as the third part of the *Ideas*. In 1788 Hamann died, and Herder seemed increasingly to assume Lessing's role defending and promoting true Enlightenment against the new dogmatism.

There is ample evidence that Herder did not fully agree with Spinoza, nor was he really a pantheist. [13] But he was intent on a *Rettung* of Spinoza, as Lessing would have called it, in order to save the memory of a great man from calumny. Herder's real project had been a comparison of Leibniz, Spinoza, and Shaftesbury. But it is symptomatic that he felt closer to Spinoza than any of the other philosophers and so was able to combine Spinoza's *Rettung* with a formulation of his own beliefs. Although Schleiermacher, Schelling, and Hegel may have surpassed Herder in their understanding of Spinoza's philosophy, Herder's little book is significant. Generally, the impact of Spinozism on German cultural life since Lessing and Herder still needs a much closer examination. [14]

God consists of five *Gespräche* (conversations). Theophron wants to remove his friend's, Philolaus's, prejudices against Spinoza, and they examine the evidence in a liberal spirit. Theophron argues that Spinoza has been maligned, especially by Pierre Bayle. It was so much easier, he claims, to read the entertaining Bayle than the difficult and obscure Spinoza; thus it is easy to understand Bayle's influence in this matter. The Cartesians were anxious to put some distance between themselves and their unwanted ally, Spinoza, Theophron contends; and, of course, the theologians fought this "atheist" and pantheist: "I am not a Spinozist, and shall never be one, but it is unbearable for me to see how the judgments of that past century of controversies on that quiet sage are repeated in our own time" (*SW*, 16:420). Theophron hands Philolaus literature on Spinoza that proves what an admirable person Spinoza was. Philolaus begins to read Spinoza's works and is surprised. Theophron counsels him to overlook the "geometrical method" that Spinoza used for his *Ethics*, since he finds this Cartesian feature not to be essential.

Thus in this first conversation, Philolaus is truly enlightened by Theophron, and the reader participates in this removal of prejudices. The two are now ready to discuss the concept of God in Spinoza's philosophy. Philolaus is troubled by Spinoza's terminology, such as his concept of substance; Theophron also criticizes Spinoza's Cartesian beliefs, for instance, that concerning spatial extension as an attribute of God (*SW*, 16:446–48). Philolaus formulates the more satisfactory principle "that the Godhead reveals itself in infinite forces in infinite manners" (16:451). Herder is happy to adduce his concept of *Kraft* (force) and thus his Leibnizian, dynamic view of the cosmos. There is no "dead matter" (16:453), and that makes both partners much more comfortable with Spinoza's system. They also contend that God and nature are not really identical in Spinoza. God is within the world and contains the world, but God and world are not interchangable. Spinoza therefore is not a real pantheist. He is not far from Leibniz's preestablished harmony. Leibniz and Spinoza would have had more plausible systems if they had had a more progressive body of scientific knowledge at their disposal, the dialogue partners think.

In the third conversation, Theophron shifts the argument to the idea of inner necessity. It is the concept of *nemesis* or *Adrastea* as the personification of the principle of measure, balance, and justice in all things. The existence and inner truth of things are based on an inner necessity that is expressed by order, harmony, and beauty (*SW*, 16:470). Herder refers to ideas of Johann Heinrich Lambert (1728–77), whom he considers the Leibniz of his age (16:469). This inner necessity or nemesis is what Theophron finds in Spinoza's concept of God. In order to "save" Spinoza, Theophron has to call his Cartesian beliefs an aberration. He saves Spinoza despite himself.

Thus he brushes aside the argument about the attributes of God, such as reason, understanding, will, and power. Herder is much less of a rationalist and really wants to make God the source and center of life and not a mathematical combination of attributes. By arguing that Spinoza came close to Leibniz, he also contends that Leibniz was close to Spinoza, a dangerous argument for the time. Herder's spokesmen agree with Spinoza in their opposition against physico-teleological proofs of God's existence and against an anthropomorphic image of God.

The fourth conversation is devoted to a close scrutiny of Lessing's words on Spinoza, as reported by Jacobi. The partners are intrigued by Lessing's *hen kai pan* (one and all), just as Herder was when he learned of it.[15] Theophron and Philolaus embark on the discussion of the highest principle or force from which others are derived. This is defined by Theophron as *das Daseyn* (being or existence) (*SW*, 16:502). They consider Lessing's speculations on Spinoza as tentative and do not pursue this matter further. They are also puzzled by the idea of a continuous expansion and contraction of God in this world. They agree that Jacobi wrongly equates Spinozism with fatalism. Determination by God's love, as in Spinoza and in the Christian religion, is fundamentally different from determination by blind fate. Fate and fatalism are associated with *Willkührlichkeit* (arbitrariness) (16:510), whereas God's determination of the course of the world is based on the highest degree of inner necessity. This inner necessity also posits a necessary relationship of Godhead and world, and thus any separation of the two, as Jacobi seems to assert, is self-contradictory. The existence of God is not "proved"; it is the premise for all reality as well as for all operations of the mind.

Now Herder is free to embark on a demonstration of his own idea of the Godhead in the fifth and concluding conversation. He adds a third participant, Theano, the woman, who sees to it that the men do not get lost in abstractions and respect concrete evidence. She is the guardian angel against "empty metaphysics" (*SW*, 16:532). Since the Godhead is defined as *Daseyn,* existence in its inner necessity and *adrastea* is the highest law of the universe. In fact *das Nichts* (nothingness) is dismissed by Theophron as an absurd impossibility. Something can never become nothing; life never ends but is merely transformed. The different levels of being are designated as forces (16:541). There is a chain of beings, and the Godhead reveals itself in everything. The Godhead is "above everything, and everything exists in it: the entire world is an expression, an appearance of His eternally living, eternally working forces" (16:542). There is a universal force called power, wisdom, or goodness, which the Godhead has communicated to creation, and thus the world bears the stamp of this goodness. The striving of each being is to be "in und für sich vollendetes Daseyn" (an existence perfect in and for itself) (16:550–51), as Theano maintains. Theophron states three laws of nature: persistence, the inner permanence of a being; union with one's own kind and separation from opposites; and becoming "similar to oneself," *Verähnlichung,* paradoxically through one's impact on others. He derives the first two laws from natural phenomena, for instance, the magnet. The third and most important law means that association, love in particular, creates similarities through interaction. Good forces leave an *Abdruck* (an imprint) in another being. Thus an influence is passed from one being to another; but the highest imprint is that of the Godhead on human beings, causing them to become more similar to God. Herder refrains from using terms like *love* and *sympathy;* he is trying to demonstrate a "natural law"; but this *Verähnlichung* (16:552) can hardly be found in physics. It is nothing else than the principle of universal love and perfectibility.

There must be perennial *Verwandlung* (metamorphosis) (*SW,* 16:567), but there cannot be death. In a world of living organisms nothing can be at rest because rest is death. The stronger a force, the more it influences others. There is no evil in this world (16:570), for evil would be *Nichts* (nothingness). Opposites, limits, transitions are called evils, but they do not deserve that name (16:570). Each substance gains its complete existence only through the union of such opposites (16:571).[16] The faults and mistakes of human beings are a motivation for higher knowledge and thus serve a good purpose (16:571). Herder discovers a "theodicy of wise necessity" (16:570); God's existence implies the idea of inner necessity and thus the idea of the best of the possible worlds. It would be absurd, though, to think that God might had chosen between alternatives. There is no arbitrariness, as nature realizes its potential by necessity.

Kant's name is never mentioned, but quite a few of the arguments are directed against him. Philolaus seems to have studied Kant.[17] Through him Herder opposes Kant's mere subjective faith in God with the idea of a direct perception of God *(Anschauung).* Certainly, intellectual proof of God's existence is impossible, but that does not mean that God's existence is not evident. Herder's world is a universe of living forces in constant transformation, eternally striving for perfection and self-realization, created and sustained by the Godhead as *Daseyn* itself. Herder is close to Goethe in this view.

Herder has been faulted for not becoming a complete Spinozist.[18] Indeed, his thought was deeply rooted in the Christian tradition, although his concept of the divinity is quite unlike the popular belief in a personal God or in the God of Deism. Herder wanted to fuse modern life science with the essence of Judeo-Christian beliefs. Most of all, in his principle of *adrastea* he found the cornerstone for his beliefs in determinism without fatalism and in order that allows for freedom. Most of all, creation wants to become more similar to the creator, and that is the ultimate meaning of all metamorphoses.

Herder's readers saw the pantheistic features of his book, that there is a divine presence in nature, working through natural laws, and blessing the creation. Goethe's *Faust* is evidence of this view.[19] Herder wanted to affirm the meaning of religion, even the Christian religion. But at the same time he introduced ideas that had to be understood in very different ways. *God*, as much as any of Herder's works, shows him as the conservative revolutionary that he was.

Palingenesis

In 1785 Herder published the first collection of what he called *Zerstreute Blätter* (Scattered leaves). The next two collections followed in quick succession, but five years passed before the fourth collection appeared in 1792, followed by the fifth and, in 1797, the sixth and last. *Scattered Leaves* was a vessel to store smaller works that Herder considered worth preserving. The similarities with the *Letters for the Advancement of Humanity* are more apparent than real. The *Letters* have a narrative framework, at least initially, and their purpose is to voice current social concerns. It was not the original idea to use them for already published material, although this happened now and then. *Scattered Leaves* makes no pretension to unity and novelty, but, strangely, shows far more unity of spirit, content, and form than the general title suggests. Herder wrote in an age of "collections," and scholarship has done little to investigate the principles of such collections, as for example, the so-called *Musenalmanache*. Goethe was fond of creating collections, and so did Jean Paul Richter, and, of course, the early romantics. There were also the *Chres-*

tomathien, florilegia, collections of the most popular aphorisms and/
or poems, which sometimes replaced the reading of the original
works. Collections with a diversity of shorter items were handy for
being read aloud in a circle of friends, a popular pastime of that
age. Collections often provide a very direct insight into the cultural
life of the era.

In his *Scattered Leaves,* Herder is openly didactic, but in an urbane
and nondogmatic manner. He has evidently both male and female
readers in mind, being perhaps more mindful of the latter. He offers
a mixture of poetry and prose, and the sequence and interconnection
of the pieces are significant. He deals with general questions of
human existence: love, beauty, death, immortality, wisdom, and
morality. Here is a humanist offering a liberal, tolerant, and fair-
minded view of fundamental questions. He also takes his readers
on the journey of discovery of new literary treasures, especially those
of Greek antiquity and the Orient. These conversations, translations,
readings, and lectures among educated and friendly people emulate
the spirit of Platonic sociability. Here are interesting items for
refined tastes. Classical Weimar may have no friendlier monument
than *Scattered Leaves.*

The editors of Herder's works have always mistreated these innocent collections. The first editors tried to rearrange them, following some hints in *Adrastea.* The Suphan edition arbitrarily
separated prose and poetry. Thus *Scattered Leaves* remain virtually
"scattered."[20]

In his first three collections, which should be considered together,
Herder offered a large choice of translations from the Greek *Anthology*
and other Greek sources, from Roman poetry (Horace and Persius),
and from Oriental legends, poems, and tales, beginning with those
of Jewish origin. In later collections he included Persian and Indian
pieces. These translations are *Nachdichtungen,* works re-creating the
spirit, but not necessarily the letter, of the original. Herder liked
conceptual poems like epigrams and fables. He was also fond of love
poetry. It is suggestive that he, who has often been called an irrationalist, had such a predilection for unequivocally didactic poetry.

Herder's essays are devoted to the appreciation of literature and
the arts, and especially to questions of life after death. Lessing's
idea of reincarnation at the end of the *Education of Mankind* had
proved to be provocative. Many passages in Herder's essays read like
dialogues with the deceased Lessing, indicating his feeling of in-

creasing loneliness, reinforced by the death of Mendelssohn and Hamann.[21] A reunion with such friends in another life would have been close to Herder's mind. He included a revised version of his commentary on Lessing's *Wie die Alten den Tod gebildet* (How the ancients depicted death) and his moving eulogy on Lessing. Although objecting to Lessing's thesis that for the ancients death had been the brother of sleep, a beautiful angel,[22] Herder rejects the skeleton as a symbol of death, along with the ideas of sin and repentance standing behind the terror of death. He handles the matter of metempsychosis cautiously and seems to try a combination of the Lutheran concept of palingenesis[24] with biogenetic principles, such as would be formulated in the nineteenth century. He stays with an inner-world idea of rebirth and metamorphosis but shrinks from a theory of biological transformation and reincarnation, although he envisions such a possibility. Perfectibility is "ennobling the soul" (*SW*, 15:303); moral betterment, rather than biological change, is called for.

Herder also included an essay on the meaning and representation of Nemesis (*SW*, 15:395–428) in Greek art and literature. Nemesis is neither a goddess of revenge nor one of justice, and it is not another Fortuna. It is the goddess of *Einhalt* (measure and restraint) (15:413), the enemy of hubris. Even *Glück* (luck and happiness) is a function of moderation, of the right measure, and not the effect of unknown powers. Nemesis is like the tongue of the scales of human affairs. It is indifferent but just. The principle of nemesis would be contrary to that of hubris.

The fourth collection is mostly devoted to the Orient, especially India. Herder had been impressed by the Indian drama *Sakuntala* (translated from English into German in a Herderian spirit and style by Georg Forster). This *Nachdichtung* can be seen as the beginning of the German romantic search for a mythical India.[24] Herder's enthusiastic review helped to launch this movement. Metempsychosis also reappears as a major topic. In *Tithon und Aurora*, Herder discusses the problem of survival beyond the appropriate time, of physical survival after spiritual death, individually and collectively. It demonstrates, as he did in the *Ideas*, the need for metamorphosis and the often stifling effect of rigid social systems. Death, for Herder, is such calcification. The inevitable question is asked: How then should change occur? As a reaction to the violent phase of the French Revolution, Herder now rejects the term "revolution," which he had previously used, and proposes "evolution" instead, that is, quiet cyclical change instead of violence (*SW*, 16:117). While he still sees some violence as unavoidable, he insists that real change, if it is to be permanent, is gradual and quiet. The din of wars, conquests, and repressions (16:117) is barbaric and futile. A healthy movement and balance of the entire society is the real recipe for the survival of a country (16:125–26), although eventually all systems have to die in order to be transformed.

With the short remark "Other times, other ideas" (*SW*, 16:131), Herder introduces the dramatic change in character of the fifth collection of 1793. He now stresses German ideas, German history, German literature, and is more openly political. He recommends Johann Valentin Andreä's (1587–1654) parables for the day and the hour, as well as his dialogues. This collection concludes with Herder's essay on Ulrich von Hutten. The fifth collection might have been more appropriate for the *Letters for the Advancement of Humanity*. Whereas the previous collections of the *Scattered Leaves* were reflections of peaceful conditions and preoccupations, the fifth collection introduces the dramatic and martial spirit of the time after 1789. Indirectly, Herder reflects on revolutionary changes in Germany, which he considered imminent. His recollections of the Thirty Years' War tried to fortify the German mind for the revolutionary events to come.

In 1797, Herder added one more collection to his *Scattered Leaves*. This time it was a somewhat nostalgic return to the themes of the earlier collections: palingenesis, Lessing's *Education of Mankind*, knowing the future before and after death. Herder offered translations of legends as well. If the previous collections expressed the social and urbane spirit of Weimar, one might almost suspect that this last collection signals a return to the status before the French Revolution. But that would be deceptive. The Weimar circle remained deeply divided, and the political problems were never far from Herder's mind. Still, the *Scattered Leaves* are not only a most characteristic product of the Herderian spirit, they also reveal something of the urbane spirit of Weimar culture, that fragile flower which did not last long, but had such an impact on modern Germany.

Chapter Five

After the Revolution

The Advancement of Humanity

Humanität was Herder's favorite word in his later years. He never really defined it, although he explained it repeatedly.[1] At the beginning of the third collection of the *Briefe zu Beförderung der Humanität* (Letters for the advancement of humanity),[2] he addresses the question again, experimenting with alternatives like *Menschheit, Menschlichkeit, Menschenwürde* (*SW,* 17:137–38). He felt, however, that the meaning of all of these words was already limited in some way, and that they would not be appropriate. *Humanität* is the essence of what is human; it is the "character of mankind" (17:138). We are all born with a potential for it. From this potential, it must be developed through education, *angebildet,* as Herder calls it, with one of his characteristic neologisms.[3] Since we cannot strive for "angelity" and should not stoop to brutality, humanity is the real goal of the human race. It is the divine spark that propels us toward *Humanität. Menschheit* or *Menschengeschlecht* designates the human race, but not that quality which is essentially human and which ought to be achieved by humans. Thus *Humanität* reveals itself in all human endeavors, especially in social and political actions, as they are intended to help fellow humans. The arts and sciences are an integral part of any advancement of humanity.

Herder's return from his journey to Italy in the summer of 1789, and his decline of the offer from the university of Göttingen, coincided with the beginning of the French Revolution. This was exciting news. Political thinking had penetrated the German middle class in an increasing degree during the last two decades before. The American War of Independence had shown that a responsible middle class could take control of its own destiny and form a republic with a representative government. American news was distributed by new journals and eagerly discussed, especially in the ubiquitous reading societies,[4] in spite of vigilant censorship. Whereas the reform-minded German middle class hoped for a gradual educational

process, the French Revolution suddenly opened the perspective of
an immediate radical change, perhaps not in the same manner as
in France, but nevertheless dramatic.[5] The fairly homogeneous educated liberal class, nobility and middle class, now broke up into
factions. Radical supporters of the new French state were opposed
by loyalists who supported the legitimate government. Most members of the educated classes were sympathetic to the French cause
and generally hopeful, but disliked violent upheavals. When the
French grew more violent and executed King Louis XVI, the mood
in Germany changed, although some of the expressions of horror
may have been more calculated than real. In this spectrum of political
tensions small groups such as the Weimar circle were caught unprepared, and friendship and tolerance suffered accordingly. Censorship was reinforced, and the police gained more power; at the
same time, the political climate in the most powerful German states—
Austria and Prussia—turned reactionary after the death of their
rulers Joseph II and Frederick II, respectively.

Peaceful Sachsen-Weimar felt the consequences of this new situation. Duke Karl August was a staunch liberal, but also a general
in the Prussian army. His trusted adviser Goethe blamed the kings
for having caused the upheavals themselves, but he resolutely supported the ancien régime and resisted the idea of abolishing small
German states in favor of a unified nation. He disliked the political
press and the rise of public opinion as an important political force.
Wieland, on the other hand, continued his journal *Der Teutsche
Merkur,* and in spite of his customary caution, even opportunism,
maintained his liberal position and sympathy for the French. Other
members of the Weimar circle, such as Friedrich von Einsiedel
(1750–1828) and Karl Ludwig von Knebel (1744–1834), were even
more outspoken, and so was Herder. Suddenly Goethe felt isolated
in Weimar and Jena, at least until he formed his alliance with
Schiller in 1794. Still, Goethe and Herder exercised restraint and
tried to preserve their friendship. This grew more difficult when
Goethe joined the duke in the Prussian campaign against France in
the fall of 1792 and participated in the siege of Mainz in 1793,
while Herder and others were openly sympathetic to the French
cause. This political climate was certainly a factor in the estrangement between Herder and Goethe, in Goethe's and Schiller's launch-
ing of the "nonpolitical" journal *Die Horen* and Herder's dispute

with Schiller,[6] thus splitting the Weimar literary life into two largely opposing camps. Herder was led through this polarization to fight Goethe's and Schiller's doctrine of *Klassik* as well as the effects of Kantianism. Most of all, the political climate was the determining factor behind the form and content of the *Letters,* ten collections of which appeared between 1793 and 1797 at the rate of two per year. They are divided into "letters," or sections, totaling 124.

Ironically, the *Letters,* the document of a divided republic of letters, claim to be the work of a group of like-minded friends of humanity. They present the image of the unified liberal class that had already been split over the current political issues. Herder, no less than Goethe, rails against the *Parteigeist* (partisan spirit) then so intensified by the attitude toward the French. Of course, he had to distance himself from any *Parteigeist* to avoid censorship and to reach his audience. He therefore builds up the fiction of a group of friends informing each other about recent or not so recent advances of humanity, and thus encouraging each other in their own work for humanity. Herder could think of certain gatherings in Weimar[7] and of modified forms of freemasonry, as models for such groupings.

In contrast to freemasonry, Herder advocates the abandonment of all secrecy. In his continuation of Lessing's *Ernst und Falk* in letter 27, at the end of the second collection, he replaces the word "Freemasons" with the "society of all thinking human beings in all parts of the world" (*SW,* 17:130). For an audience that had had experience with freemasonry and knew Lessing's provocative dialogues, this was a clear signal. The *Letters* advocate an open forum on public matters and strive for a society where everybody can participate in public affairs; but they clearly bear the imprint of the constraints of the ancien régime and its narrow limits.

In 1791 Herder had published the fourth part of the *Ideas.* For the fifth part, he had to think of the three momentous changes: the rule of the barbaric Nordic peoples under the spiritual domination of Catholicism, the Reformation, taken in a broad sense, and, finally, the French Revolution, which marked the inception of a true European Republic. According to Herder, the goals of Luther's Reformation, which were the return to Jesus Christ's religion and the liberation of the people, had been subverted by the German princes. These same princes—their descendants of course—were now resisting the new liberation of the people that had begun in France. For conveying such a view, although cautiously, the loose form of *Letters* seemed more appropriate than the format of the *Ideas*. When Herder was drafting the first two collections of the *Letters* in 1792, he still wanted to say openly what he thought, namely, that a republican form of government would be better for France than a constitutional monarchy (*SW*, 18:317) and that the French were on the right track, in spite of many shortcomings. It is hard to tell how much of this material would have been published; but the execution of Louis XVI on 21 January 1793 made a direct defense of the French Republic impossible. Herder's published *Letters* bear little resemblance to his original plans. They exhibit hesitation, caution, and a very indirect "slave language" of double meanings, allusions, and omissions. When the first collections reached Goethe and Karl August, who were fighting the French in Mainz, they were relieved to find nothing really objectionable in the *Letters*.

Even in their amputated and self-censored form, the *Letters* leave no doubt about the liberal outlook of their author. They also betray the confusion of the time. Herder had never been a friend of King Frederick II and would not have considered living under his rule; but now he praised the dead king and quoted extensively from his letters to show how a great mind was working. He is equally complimentary to Emperor Joseph II, whose reforms and German policies had been controversial. Of course, these rulers had inferior successors who ruined what they had achieved. Herder's praise implies criticism. Austrian censorship, the "best" in the German states, saw through this scheme and banned the sale of the book in Austria.

Likewise, Herder's praise of Benjamin Franklin, placed at the beginning of the book, had to be taken as a political signal. After all, Franklin was identified with the great republic in America. Herder's discussion of the role of poetry in public affairs, although much more hesitant and cautious than previous statements, and his ideas about French revolutionary literature (*SW*, 18:321–22),[8] were meant as a reminder to rulers. The nation-building aspect of Luther's reformation was emphasized, again an indirect plea against the status quo and for a unified German nation. Herder also wants Lessing's *Emilia Galotti* performed on a regular basis for the political education of the German audience. Beside such examples, Herder discusses his basic concepts: *Humanität*, the perfectibility of humankind, and his phrase *Geist der Zeit* (spirit of the age).

The "patriotic" spirit still prevails in the later collections; but they lose some of the original drive and sometimes degenerate into sequences of loosely connected items. Stressing the moral content and obligation of authors, Herder offers a fragmentary history of literature from ancient Greece to the present. His hero is Lessing, and his faint praise of Goethe (*SW*, 18:123) in the eighth collection betrays hostility: Goethe's works are characterized by a *teilnahmslose*, an "indifferent accurate description of things which are visible and an active depiction of his characters" (18:123). Thus Goethe has the talent of a great artist, he is the master of all forms; but does he really contribute to the advancement of humanity as Lessing had done? Herder is also cool to his friend Wieland and hardly mentions Schiller. It would be hard to detect in Herder's picture of German literature that this was a period of the highest achievements and of seminal new ideas. Clearly Herder was a bitter man at that point and grossly unfair in his judgment. He clearly prefers Klopstock, Lessing, and lesser lights of the last generation, such as Ewald von Kleist, Gleim, Gessner, and Hölty, to his contemporaries.

Herder is on much more solid ground with his polemics against the remnants of *Gallicomanie,* castigating the taste of the small courts in Germany. It is a battle he should have fought when he was young, and by praising Lessing he once more condemns Goethe, the court poet. Herder still fights for his goal, the great German national literature that expresses the spirit of the nation for the advancement of humanity. He condemns Goethe and Schiller because they seem to write *l'art pour l'art* and shy away from social obligations. They also give bad examples to the young generation of romantics, who must have looked too esoteric for Herder. To be sure, Herder was ready to acknowledge talent in a younger writer, as in the case of Jean Paul Richter, who in turn received unfair treatment by Goethe;[9] but, on the whole, he was neither fair nor forward looking.

Herder was reluctant to talk openly about *Rückschritte* (regressions), but in the tenth collection he finally confronted the issue. Again the condemnation of European conquests and the destructive consequences of colonization is clear: wars that are not in self-defense are condemned. True patriotism means respect for other countries; nationalism and cosmopolitism are by no means opposites. Herder foresees the possibility of an "alliance of all educated nations" (*SW,* 18:271), exhibiting enlightened self-respect and respect for others. This alliance should oppose all transgressors against mankind.

What in Herder's view is the optimal form of government? While,

on principle, the republican form is best (18:283), historical and
cultural conditions might favor another solution. There is no one
form of government that can be ideal for all times (18:283). While
human beings cannot know the goal of history, they are still ob-
ligated to do the right thing and thus contribute to a better life in
the future (18:286). Contrary to what Kant—who is not mentioned—had said, there is no radical evil force on earth. Since
"Christianity demands the purest humanity in the purest manner"
(18:301), the notion of evil does not belong in the Christian religion.
For Herder the religion of Jesus is still the purest form and incar-
nation of *Humanität,* for it preaches universal love and mutual assistance. Thus for Herder Christian missionaries and Teutonic knights
can make a mockery of this humanity and are evidence of regression.
The Christian church has not yet caught up with Jesus Christ.

The original theme of the *Letters*—the French Revolution—is
never mentioned. Kant and Kantianism are omitted, although Herder had planned to discuss them. Herder focuses on his great political
ideal, the Republic of Europe as a federation of nation states, but
in an indirect way. He returns to his favorite theme of *litterature
engagée,* of the social and moral functions and obligations of literature.
Instead of criticizing his former friend Goethe for shunning such
responsibilities, however, he gives him faint and insincere praise.
He felt that he had to speak out; but he did not know precisely
how frank he could be. It is regrettable from our vantage point that
Herder vacillated between courage and caution, between large perspectives and petty quarrels. But this may reflect his circumstances
and the condition of the German republic of letters. Herder was
opposed to Schiller's concept of "aesthetic education," but he does
not actually refer to it. Schiller and Goethe were right in feeling
uncomfortable when reading the *Letters,* which helped them to disregard Herder's valid criticism of their position.

The *Letters* are the first work of Herder's last decade, often called
a period of "decline." The recent "rehabilitation" of the late Herder
is far from complete,[10] and it would be foolish to deny certain
weaknesses in his last works. However, he was not merely dis-
gruntled, as Goethe made others believe, but fighting for causes he
believed in. He was hindered by his surroundings and the circumstances, as the *Letters* show more clearly than any other work. Perhaps
he should have written the *Letters* as he planned them, and kept
them in the drawer for posterity; but that was not Herder's notion

of the duties of a writer. Also, he wavered in his evaluation of the French Revolution and the permissible amount of violence. Although he did by no means share Goethe's reverence for order as such, Herder was at times unsure how much should be said in public that was critical of existing powers. The Revolution did put severe strains on the ideal of *Humanität*. Did it indeed advance humanity or, rather, *Bestialität?*

Still, at a time when German states tried to make themselves immune to progress, Herder maintained the spirit of the advancement of *Humanität* and gave encouraging and comforting examples. It is true that, in these letters, significant insights alternate with less significant ones and some rather regrettable passages. The *Letters* are still important in two ways: as a barometer of the political climate in Germany in these years, and last but not least, as a substitute for the missing fifth part of the *Ideas*, whose fragments are scattered in it.

Christianity

Herder had followed with keen interest the heated debate over the *Fragments* published by Lessing, and he had urged Lessing to publish Reimarus's entire work. Not that he agreed with it in any way. He certainly did not think that miracles such as the resurrection were tricks and deception, for he thought that the Bible text contained the honest truth as the writers perceived it at the time. Herder shared Lessing's view that the religion of Jesus Christ and his immediate followers, St. John in particular, was fundamentally different from the dogmatic and political religion of the Christian churches. In his sermons, he tried to distill the essence of Christianity from the gospels and epistles in a nondogmatic, ecumenical way. Jesus Christ was for him the embodiment of *Humanität,* and in that sense Herder's world view was indeed a "Christian Humanism."[11] But the formula may have appeared tautological to Herder himself. Maybe it would be more appropriate to speak of a "Humanistic Christianism," always keeping in mind Herder's concept of *Humanität*. As the concluding part—and, as he felt, crowning achievement—of his religious writings, Herder now offered a series of treatises that he himself called *Christliche Schriften* (Christian writings) that dealt with the New Testament, Jesus Christ, and religion in general.

The *Christian Writings* appeared in five collections between 1794 and 1798. It is good to keep in mind how many different things Herder was doing at a given time. The late Herder obviously liked the term *Sammlung,* which he used for the concurrent *Scattered Leaves* and the *Letters for the Advancement of Humanity.* While Herder insisted on the notion of *Ganzheit,* he rejected rigorous and abstract systems. It would be interesting to speculate how a crowning synthesis of all of his works may have looked—another *Sammlung?* Herder was then becoming more aphoristic in his style with age, just like Goethe or Jean Paul; but it may seem surprising for the effusive Herder that he could be terse.

The *Christian Writings,* however, are not really "collections." They are clear, concise, frank, and straightforward treatises and are evidently a labor of love, written in a fairly peaceful mood and in quick succession, although polemics are not absent. Obviously, one of their goals is to combat Kantianism. The *Christian Writings* address a general audience of (mostly) nonchurchgoers. Herder disliked printed sermons and—unfortunately—never made a collection of his own, but the spirit and style of his sermons is clearly discernible in these writings, which are a confession of faith. He believed that the noblest religion in history had been taught and exemplified by Jesus Christ. While Christianity had degenerated in barbaric ages, the message of the Bible was there for everybody to receive. It was mandatory, then, to enter into the spirit of the original text and the attitude of the first Christians. Herder mustered his philological acumen, historical and anthropological intuition, and common sense to examine the Bible text, assuming the subjective veracity and trustworthiness of its writers. He felt that the gospel accounts were, of course, far from perfect. The Greek of these writers was far from native or literary; they may have erred in what they heard and wanted to believe. These are human documents, and Jesus Christ, as Herder never tired of repeating, was the *Menschensohn,* who came to live on this earth to experience *Menschlichkeit* and *Humanität.* The very human imperfection of the gospels gives them a stamp of authenticity and makes them plausible in the context of their situation.

Herder goes on to explain some of the points most vigorously attacked by the author of the *Fragments.* [12] For instance, he uses sober psychology and straightforward philological interpretations to explain the "speaking in tongues" afer the Pentacostal miracle, guarding himself against groundless religious enthusiasm and fanaticism and denying the association of early Christianity with *Schwärmerei.* St. Paul's epistles show how careful the early Christians were not to make it a habit to be "moved by the spirit," even if it happened to some of them. Herder soberly traces the belief in resurrection or rebirth to Judaism. He believed that Jesus was gone from his grave, and that he reappeared in the flesh and associated with his disciples. The disciples saw him, and they have to be believed. But even the gospels contain later additions that have to be discarded to reach the earliest layers. Certainly, the early Christians believed that the end of the world was near, and they adjusted their lives accordingly.

The central part of Herder's *Christian Writings* was his account of the life of Jesus. In examining the three synoptic gospels, Matthew, Mark, and Luke, it was obvious that there were both connections and marked differences between them. The question of a common source had to be raised (*SW, 19:141*). Mark, Herder contended, must have relied on St. Peter's oral stories; neither he nor St. Luke can have been firsthand eyewitnesses. The gospels are genuine writings of Christians of Jewish origin and were written down in the second half of the first century (19:147). Of course, it is a historical accident that these four gospels, and no others, were preserved and canonized.

Still, the gospels contain some uncontroversial facts about Jesus. He was a man of thirty years who appeared at the Jordan wanting to be baptized by John the Baptist. After the baptism an aura formed, indicating that he was blessed and chosen by God. He then went into the desert to fast, and later formed a small group of disciples. He taught them more by his example than by particular doctrines. He wanted to *anbilden* (form) his religion, not *einlehren* (indoctrinate) (*SW, 19:169*). Herder downplays the particular miracles that Jesus performed, but insists on the central message that He was Christ the son of God. Jesus had an internalized faith in God and a love for all fellow human beings. He was opposed to rigorous rules and the ceremonies of the Jewish ritual. He spoke of a spiritual kingdom, whereas the prophets had foretold the reestablishment of a strong Jewish state. The Jews, waiting for the coming Messiah, had to find Jesus wanting; they thought he was blasphemous and dangerous. He himself knew that he would be persecuted. Herder places all of this in the historical context—the Jewish tradition and the political situation—while trying to give the appropriate interpretation to the words. Why in Herder's opinion were the gospels written, and what function did they have for the early Christians? They were histories, reminding the faithful that Jesus was Christ, that he had been crucified, resurrected, had gone back to heaven, and that he would come again at the end of time. Jesus was a very human person while he was on earth: witness his humility, his hesitation before accepting his mission, his practical wisdom, his jokes, and his emotions. By describing the lives of the early Christians and the role of the apostles, Herder wants to show that the evangelists look like simple, straightforward, trustworthy people, and that what they tell sounds plausible. Herder does not wish to "prove" anything. It could be argued that by humanizing Jesus he really continues the road from Reimarus to David Friedrich Strauss.[13] But that argument would miss Herder's paradox that Jesus' *Humanität* underscores his divine nature and mission. The suffering, death, and resurrection of Jesus opened the eyes of the apostles for the message that Jesus was not a king in a worldly sense, but that his kingdom was from another world. That is the guidepost so often missed by the Christian churches.

St. John's gospel must have been written later than the others, Herder surmises, probably when the apostle was old. John must have known about other writings on Jesus. He wanted to take the story of Christ out of the confining Palestinian context and not only interpret (*erläutern*) the myth, but purify (*läutern*) it (*SW*, 19:264). Herder comments at length on the Oriental traditions, on Plato and Neoplatonism and on Gnostic myths that must have been known to John, who wanted to counter them with his laconic statements on the *logos* in the beginning of his story. This first chapter of John's gospel, which has generated so much dissension, was designed to unite Christians against wrong metaphysics and mythologies. John is Herder's second hero after Jesus. In John's religion, God is light, and there is no darkness in Him. God is love, and whoever remains in that love remains in God, and God within him (19:353). John is not telling a story; he is teaching truth, love, and the bond of a real community.

The harmonization of the four gospels, as it had been tried so many times, seems pointless for Herder. The gospels were written on the basis of oral tradition, and while they contain points fundamental for all Christians, they do not tell all the details of Jesus' life. They agree that Jesus was baptized, crucified, and resurrected, that he was Christ, the son of God; but for the rest they aimed at different audiences.

In the fourth and fifth collections, Herder asks more general questions. What is the spirit of Christianity? What is religion, as opposed to doctrines and rituals? The two treatises are short. They are filled with messages of truth, love, and communal care, and they are no less fervent than Lessing's last writings in their attack on institutional dogmatism in the name of Christian love. Coming from a high church official, they are remarkable documents.

The words of the Bible, Herder maintains, are simple and natural: they are taken from the Jewish tradition and from the everyday language of the time. Rendered obscure by the mystifications of later doctrines, they have caused a variety of dogmatic disputes. When the sources are examined in their own spirit, such disputes dissolve. Take, for instance, the Holy Spirit. Spirit is the vital force in life, that which moves people. Different meanings may be given to the word, but to derive dogmas from personifications and allegories is futile and dangerous.

Thus the text has to be understood in natural terms, and it is our task to draw conclusions from it for our own lives. Christianity is not an intellectual system to be contemplated. To understand Christ is to follow Christ, to live like a Christian, in love and *Billigkeit* (liberality) (*SW*, 20:46), and in a communal spirit. Christianity is a *Gemeinschaft* (community) devoted to spiritual truth and love; but it also has to be a *Gesellschaft* (society) (20:101) and thus shares in the imperfections of all human institutions. If Christianity is integrated into a state government, either the state will absorb the religion, or religion will undermine the state. The two of them are not compatible (20:101). Herder's thought is clearly in the heretic strain, but distinctly modern in his advocacy of the separation of religion and state. If one translates the spirit of early Christianity into contemporary life, one also translates the word of the Bible, as Luther had done. This would mean to "germanize" the old Judaism (20:99). (No anti-Semitism should be read into this statement.) Herder was convinced that Christianity grew out of Judaism in decay, and that the Christian religion had to surpass the confines of Palestinian Jewry in order to come into its own. Christian language had to change by transforming itself into different cultures and ages, even if the spirit remained the same. The original texts

are in need of such translation, which is also a liberation from later
rigid dogmatism. Herder praises St. John and St. Paul, but deplores
the influence of St. Augustine on his own Lutheran church.
Herder's books are not just for Christians. His concept of religion
is truly universal and adamantly opposed to dogmatism: "If religion
distinguishes itself from dogmata *(Lehrmeinungen)*, it grants a place
to each of them without wishing to be dogma. Dogmata separate
and embitter, whereas religion unites; for in the hearts of all human
beings it is only one and the same" *(SW,* 20:135). Truth is the
same in all human minds (20:136). Religion is simple, as is exemplified by the religion of Jesus. Herder offers explanations for
what he considers the true and simple meaning of "God the father,"
the savior Jesus Christ, the Holy Ghost, and the meaning and
purpose of baptism and the commemoration of the Last Supper. He
finds the roots for many superstitions, as he calls dogmatic traditions, in Oriental mysticism, in Jewish rituals, in magic beliefs, or
simply in intellectualizing trends. He wants to have a "pure" Christian religion, which may be a concept not too far removed from
that of "natural religion," although Herder insists on Jesus the savior
and the historical foundation of Christianity. For Herder rebirth
after death, a metamorphosis of life forces, is a natural phenomenon.
   Herder may have been at least partially blind when he considered
the philosophy of religion of Kant and his idealistic followers Fichte
and Schelling a new dogmatism. He was certainly allergic to too
much intellectualizing. His central concept is *glauben,* which for
him meant an inner conviction, very different from *meinen* (to have
an opinion). The inner conviction of religion, based on creditable
teaching and tradition, is different from scientific knowledge. Science may ultimately prove the great harmony of God's creation, but
it uses its own methods irrespective of such religious truth. There
will be many scientific discoveries that seem to contradict the religious view, but one has to take things in a wider perspective.
Religion should never "theologize" with each wing of a gnat; it
should not moralize with each individual historical event. Herder
comes back to his fundamental belief in God, the creator and per-
server of the world *(All-Erhalter, pantokrator) (SW,* 20:153); Jesus
Christ, the *Heilbringer,* the savior (20:166); the Holy Spirit which
is the heavenly spiritual support in a holy community (20:180).
Religion proves itself in action; universal love and spiritualization
bring the human race closer to God, making it divine through

developing *Humanität*. The consequences of religion for social behavior are evident: Mankind ought to be united in love; the love of God ought to be the model of behavior for social groups within the group and among different groups. Freedom means adherence to the laws of nature; and love, not arbitrariness, should bring about order and harmony. Human beings are not second makers; they should not try to re-create the world in their own image, least of all as a machine.

Herder defends religion. He sees a dangerous transfer of divine authority to substitute gods created by man: the churches, state governments, princes, scientific or ideological dogmatism, etc. This struggle against dogmatism is double-edged, like most of Herder's fights. He combats the vestiges of past superstitions in the dogmata and ceremonies of the Christian churches; but he also opposes secularization. Herder seems often conservative, if not hostile to progress, at this point. In his struggle against dogmatism, he wanted to free the world for religion, not from religion; and it looked sometimes as if he condemned those who had the same goal but followed different paths. Herder, however, was convinced that the crisis of his age was fundamentally a crisis of religion, and that secularization would only create new superstitions. Thus he was, once again, both the heir and the critic of the Enlightenment.

Herder believed that the Christian religion was *Menschenreligion,* a religion for all mankind. Contrary to what Lessing seemed to think in his *Education of Mankind,* no new religion needed to be invented, but mankind should base its future on the essentials of the religion of Jesus Christ. Herder found good seeds in most religious beliefs; but he adhered to the universality of his—nondogmatic—Christian faith. This should be considered a remarkable position for a Christian clergyman and church official. It is a truly humanistic Christian outlook.

Metacritique

When Herder first looked at Kant's *Critique of Pure Reason,* he decided not to read it. Hamann, however, did not stop rereading it and bombarded Herder with questions. Hamann went back to other philosophers, especially David Hume, and drafted different versions of a review that he labeled "Metacritique." Herder, while sympathetic to Hamann's fruitless efforts, did not get involved. He

was writing his *Ideas.* Then came Kant's harsh attack on the first
and second part of the *Ideas.* Still, Herder, while beginning to attack
some of Kant's positions, never mentioned him by name, and even
in the *Letters for the Advancement of Humanity,* where he had planned
to warn against the dangers of Kantianism, he inserted a moving
passage that shows how the memory of Kant, the teacher, was dear
to him.[14] Herder may have had many faults; but he was a loyal
friend. Increasingly, he noticed the influence of Kantianism on the
younger generation, and its application to art theory, for instance
in Schiller's writings. He finally felt compelled to react; yet he did
not want to attack Kant, the man, who was old by that time, but
the principles of his philosophy, which he considered wrong. The
students at the university of Jena learned atheism from this philosophy, and they also learned that the arts were not concerned with
social and moral values. Herder's counterattack had two main tar-
gets: the epistemological approach of the *Critique of Pure Reason* and
the aesthetic theory of the *Critique of Judgment.* He attacked the first
in his *Metakritik,* the second in his *Kalligone.*

He called the first part of his metacritique *Verstand und Erfahrung:
Eine Metakritik zur Kritik der reinen Vernunft* (Understanding and
experience: a metacritique of the *Critique of Pure Reason*), whereas
the second part was called *Vernunft und Sprache* (Reason and Language). The second point, reason and language *(logos)* is what Hamann had had in mind. Hamann, who was long dead when Herder
wrote the *Metacritique,* had sent him a draft of his abortive "Metacritique." It is not clear whether Herder reread this typically
Hamannian short rhapsody before or while writing his book. A
disciple of Kant named Rink unearthed a copy of Hamann's "Metacritique" during the controversy—and after the publication of
Herder's book—and called Herder a "plagiarizer" of Hamann. In
his response Herder may have overstated Hamann's part in this
venture because their approach is radically different.[15] No direct
quotes from Hamann can be detected in Herder's book, and Hamann
may have been as indebted to Herder for his ideas as vice versa.[16]
Herder's only specific debt to Hamann may have been the happy
coinage of the word *Metakritik.*

The Kantians knew that Herder was a serious adversary, so they
were happy to add the argument of plagiarism to their main argument that Herder had completely misunderstood Kant. Kant and
Kantianism have permeated German cultural life to such a degree

that Herder has never been forgiven for his *Metacritique,* while *Kalligone* has found a few champions.[17]

A reevaluation of Herder's *Metacritique* would, of course, lie outside the scope of this brief introduction. Haym is correct to insist on the following basic points: Herder and Kant speak different languages. Herder refuses to enter into the spirit of Kant's system, and he rejects Kant's terminology. He criticizes from the outside and opposes one system by another system (Herder was, of course, allergic to the term "system"). Herder found weaknesses in Kant's *Critique* that have also been found by others. Herder's work does not really provide a critique of the *Critique;* it is most interesting as a statement of Herder's own position. Unfortunately, Herder's negative attitude makes it difficult to separate genuine critique from satire.[18]

Other interesting features should be added. Whenever Herder agrees with Kant, he points out that Kant's ideas are not really his own but those of Leibniz, Locke, Hume, Lambert, and others. This belittling of Kant's achievement is contrary to Herder's usual approach. His anger lets him forget his customary liberality. Jean Paul Richter, who shared Herder's opposition against Kantianism (not Kant) and wrote a real satire, the *Clavis Fichtiana,* against it, tried in vain to convert Herder's anger into reasoning. Herder invoked English philosophy, especially Locke and Berkeley, in his fight against Kantianism. Herder's brand of empiricism is, of course, a product of the pre-Kantian philosophical discussion, which was cut off by Kant's and Fichte's enormous influence. Their contemporaries were then degraded to "popular" or "school" philosophers, but Lambert, Johannes Nikolaus Tetens (1736–1807), Ernst Platner (1744–1818), Moses Mendelssohn, and quite a few others should not have been dismissed so lightly.

Herder insists that being *(das Seyn)* has to be accepted as the precondition for any thinking, and that it is wrong to be absorbed by the operations of the human mind, as Kant seems to be. *Das Seyn* manifests itself in forces and in spatial and temporal dimensions such as duration. Basic terms, for Herder, reveal basic experiences. In his view, a priori notions are impossible because they would be empty abstractions. Such basic notions as time and space constitute themselves with and through the constitution of human experience. Cognition is not *Erkennen,* but *Anerkennen.* This recognition is also termed *Innewerden.* Kant had used *Anschauung,* but *Anschauung,* Herder argues, is derived from the visual sense only. Sensation, however, means derivation from all sources through all our senses. The sense of hearing is related to the sequence of events, that is, to time; while space and time, seeing and hearing, are connected by living forces. Herder does not agree with Kant's transcendental deduction of his notions of human understanding. He argues against the term "transcendental" as he had argued against the term "a priori" or Kant's use of the words "synthetic" and "analytic." Herder posits the original being and sees the role of reason in finding unity in diversity and in the recognition of a given reality. For him Kant's problem with idealism and realism, with *noumenon* and *phenomenon*, appearance and the thing in itself, is mere wordplay. Herder was not bothered by the fact that he had to assume, as in *Of Cognition and Sensation*, that there had to be an analogy between the human mind and the reality inside and around the human beings. The human mind, Herder insists, does not construe the world outside, it merely recognizes it, albeit in human terms. Reason cannot recognize the world without previous active experience and involvement. Thus Herder does not go beyond the spheres of history, nature, and psychology. Going beyond the analysis of experience, in his opinion, is like going into *Nichts* (nothingness). Subsequently, nihilism would become a catchword hurled against Kantian idealism, first by Friedrich Heinrich Jacobi.[19]

Herder argues against Kant's entire book and against every detail. Obviously he can be neither fair nor just. He quotes Kant extensively and seems to provide nothing but a commentary; but he actually quotes and rejects. It would have made Herder's case more convincing if he had stated his position in positive terms and pointed out his fundamental differences with Kant. Why follow Kant step by step if one disagrees with each of these steps anyway? Did he really think he could convince Kantians in this manner? None of Herder's friends, who agreed with his stance, was happy with his strategy.

Herder took his basic categories, such as *Sein* and *Kraft,* not from mathematics and physics, but from the life sciences. With the initial recognition of *Sein,* philosophy becomes ontology, and the constitution of knowledge can be investigated in psychological and historical terms. Herder was not a "philosopher" asking probing questions like Kant. He was, rather, anxious to stay on the secure ground of commonsense reality. Thus, even apart from his ill will toward Kant, he could not see much sense in Kant's a priori reasoning, his categories, and his deduction. Whereas Jacobi and Jean Paul, among many others, were deeply troubled by the implications of Kant's position, Herder was personally unconcerned.

Scholars agree that Herder was on philosophically more secure ground when he wrote *Kalligone,* the metacritique of the *Critique of Judgment.* He was not only cognizant of aesthetic theory, but also had a rich experience of creativity and enjoyment in the arts. He had seen great examples of architecture, sculpture, and paintings in France and especially in Italy; and he was as familiar with world literature as any of his contemporaries. Herder was able to argue that certain statements of Kant were contrary to common knowledge of those who actually enjoyed the arts. Kant, it seems, knew little about music, and had a minimal exposure to the visual arts and a less than adequate knowledge of and taste in literature.

It was not hard for Herder to attack and correct a good number of statements in Kant's *Critique.* Herder's ill will was still apparent in giving the worst possible interpretation to what Kant was saying. Some of Herder's objections are, however, significant. Again, *Kalligone* commands more interest as a restatement of Herder's own convictions than as a critical commentary on Kant. Typical is Herder's critique of Kant's use of the terms *Spiel* (play) and the attribute *interesselos* (impartial). Since Herder considered literature and the arts a most serious, respectable, socially needed activity, he chose to take Kant's definition as a relegation of the arts to a mere pastime, to be received without real interest. This is not what Kant meant, but Herder wanted to make his point. He also found reasons to criticize Kant's differentiation between crafts subservient to customers' needs and the arts free from such considerations. Do such arts produce only luxury items and playthings for people who are bored and need entertainment? Herder insisted that art was the work of genius and could not be constrained by rules and conventions; but art should have real significance for the community and not be an idle plaything. Herder differed much less from Kant than is apparent in his assessment of the creative process,[20] but he stressed again and again the dignity and social meaning of artistic creations. Beauty created by the artist was, in fact, the recognition of beauty in nature, and therefore meaningful. Herder goes at length into the details of *Naturschönheit* (natural beauty) in minerals, plants, and animals, and the proportions and expressions of the human being.

Great art is the re-creation of the beauty imbedded in the order of the cosmos.

Vollkommenheit is the ideal of art, which is the expression of the inner perfection ingrained in each form or organism. Art recognizes this ideal of inner perfection, and thus expresses the natural laws and the goodness of creation. It therefore expresses *Adrastea,* the right measure in things and events. With this ideal of art, the sublime and the beautiful cannot be opposites; for the sublime is the beautiful in its utmost dimension. Herder harmonizes and synthesizes where Kant analyzes and differentiates. Whereas Kant was, in truth, speaking about the arts as an ornament of social life, Herder considers the arts an expression of the inner harmony of the cosmos. Grace and measure are general basic principles for the perfection of human life. Herder never ceases to think of ancient Greece. We are most interested in the aesthetic sphere, he maintains, but it is interest without *Eigennutz* (egotistical considerations). *Spiel,* he argues against Kant and Schiller, cannot improve the moral fiber of the human being; it is without obligations. Mindful of Shaftesbury, Herder, who wants the human being to become more similar to God, sees beauty as an integral part in this endeavor. He never separates aesthetic and moral values, and upholds his ideal of *Kalokagathia* sometimes in a stubborn, even shortsighted way. But he is justified in focusing on the problem of the meaning of the arts for real life. However Goethe and Schiller, and the young romantics under their influence, refused to acknowledge the problem and treated Herder's ideas as retrogressive.

Neither the *Metacritique* nor *Kalligone* is pleasant or easy reading. The reader is easily lost in the thicket of details and polemics. Herder's wide perspectives seem to disappear behind bitterness and petty quarrels. Herder writes his books not against a man, but against a philosophy, as he puts it; but he may have lost the right measure. Herder felt isolated and threatened; he was right in considering the impact of Kantianism decisive. Presented with more detachment, his arguments would have been more valid—but that is easy to say from a safe distance. Herder's fight for empiricism and for the relevance of the arts should, however, not be underestimated. The books contain quite a few "seeds" still relevant today, and it would be fatal to reduce his arguments to a mere personal quarrel.

Adrastea

Herder's last years were overshadowed by frequent illness, numerous problems in his large family, and dissension in his Weimar environment. The attempted reconciliation with Goethe never really took place, and Duke Karl August became angry when Herder obtained a Bavarian patent of nobility for purely practical reasons. Herder's literary feuds, mostly of his own making, hurt his sensibilities; he felt isolated and approached the new century with apprehension. This new century allowed him two achievements that had an opposite fate: he translated, or rather adapted, Spanish romances on the *Cid* that became by far his most popular nineteenth century work; and his swan song as a commentator of his age and on history, *Adrastea,* found little recognition and was soon forgotten. His readers had begun to desert him with the *Letters for the Advancement of Humanity.* While the metacritical works had a kind of *succès de scandale,* the response to his last works was mostly *Schweigen* (silence), as he termed it himself. His former readers had other concerns now; or perhaps these works did not measure up to the expectations raised by works like the *Ideas.* It is interesting to note that Herder's translations and not only the *Cid,* proved popular. Jean Paul Richter had suggested a journal aimed against Kantianism and *Klassik,* chiefly to be directed by Herder, Jacobi, and himself. Herder had toyed with this "Aurora" project as a private enterprise. Finally, he renamed it *Adrastea,* and it became a new vessel for collections in the manner of the *Letters for the Advancement of Humanity.* Herder would not have been a capable editor. He placed a high value on this project and continued it with all his failing forces, possibly sacrificing his health to the elusive completion of the book. He wanted to give an assessment of the achievements of the just ended eighteenth century. Measured against such expectations, *Adrastea* is clearly disappointing in most of its sections. The early critics were right in feeling that there were too many details, even verbiage at times, obscuring the important points that Herder wanted to make. *Adrastea* shares some of the faults of the *Letters:* Herder is not always straightforward and frank, and he skirts central issues in favor of tangential ones; moreover, his view of the past century is not always impartial.

Herder included his own poetic works, especially those in dramatic form, in his new collections. These works, while interesting, suffer from a comparison with Schiller's and Goethe's dramas of the period, such as Herder himself invites. Herder was still a great man and writer, but sometimes the bathos of the environment caught up with him, as it did with Goethe and Schiller.

Adrastea appeared in "volumes," each divided into two parts. Between 1801 and 1803, Herder completed five such volumes; a sixth was added by his son after his death. The guiding principle for this considerable amount of material was "truth and justice," judging events by the criterion of the right measure. This principle implies that each action causes a proportionate reaction; the wars of King Louis XIV aroused the fear of his possible domination of Europe. With the criterion of the right measure, Herder can examine the two sides of a phenomenon and try to find a fair evaluation. Sometimes, however, he presents the opposite sides without any synthesis. For example, he explains the greatness of Jonathan Swift, arguing for the dignity of satirical poetry. But he also describes Swift's limitations, which he attributes to the adverse times and to his difficult life. The satirist now appears as a victim of his age, and satire as a product of an age in crisis. The antithesis in this case appears to be stronger than the thesis.

Herder is still opposed to state churches and praises John Locke's fight for religious freedom. Herder's criticism of England must have been colored by recent events; he still hopes for the progress for mankind to come from France. Once more, he condemns court poetry, as opposed to real poetry that emanates from the people. The flexible form of *Adrastea* gives Herder the opportunity to inquire into the nature of literary forms, such as aphorism, didactic poem, fable, idyl, fairy tale, novel, and theater and drama. Since Adrastea is his principle, drama must be his prime exemplification of fate in poetry. He offers interpretations of Greek tragedy, Shakespeare, and Lessing. Schiller and Goethe are condemned through silence. Herder also branches out into the history of science, offers a critique of Christian missionaries and colonization, and discusses freemasonry, epic poetry, the German language, and criticism. He summarizes and clarifies previous statements, but he also emphasizes the historical context. *Adrastea* is significant as a contribution to cultural, specifically literary, history. Herder remains liberal and equitable, as long as he stays away from objects of his anger. He is able to be fair to Wesley's methodism. He staunchly defends freethinkers, but categorically rejects Mandeville's fable and its implications.

A little noticed section under the heading "Atlantis" (*SW*, 164–76) contains Herder's proposals for a better organization of society. The central issue is how to make better use of intellectuality and spiritual forces for the good of society. Herder surprises his readers by asking for *Aufsicht* over the universities (24:166). He approves of organizations like the Jesuits or the Pietist community in Herrnhut. This supervision must be in capable hands. If the ruler cannot exercise it, it should be delegated to a commission. While stimulating and encouraging the best talents, the state should organize and control the curriculum.

Herder disliked most of the criticism of books practiced at the time. Certainly, the state should not censure publications but have the authority to criticize. This would be the proper role for academies of sciences, which could be "tribunals" for publications (*SW*, 24:169). Critics should be the most dignified members of society. Herder fights against a bad system of education where professors teach what they please, and against inferior criticism that reinforces pernicious writings that flood the market. The state ought to promote beneficial writings and prepare the population for new, progressive measures of government. Herder tries to fight books that might exert a bad influence, and he also thinks that control of the theaters is necessary. He grants freedom to argue about doctrines and religious ceremonies, but not about the essence of religion itself. As much as possible, he wants to encourage rather than coerce.

Still, while all these restrictions may have made sense, given the experiences of Herder's last years, such measures would sound very dangerous after the experiences of the last two centuries. Herder trusted the civil servants more than the university professors, the journalists, and especially the churches. True, the civil servants were among the most progressive and enlightened classes at the time; but Herder's habitual distrust of state power stands in curious contrast to such proposals. Herder is clearly concerned about *Independentismus* (*SW*, 24:168) generated by the French Revolution and by the wave of Kantianism. After years of negative experiences with chaotic freedom, he finally joins Goethe in his preference for order and positive thinking.

Once more, Herder fights on two fronts at once. Absolutism had

spent itself; its enforced class separation prevented the free inter-
change which ensures the life of the social body (*SW*, 24:174). This
separation prevented the most capable people from fulfilling their
potential for the good of the entire society. Lessing never found his
proper place (24:172), nor did Herder. But if the ideal of *das Wahre,
Schöne und Gute* (24:176) is to be realized, it should not be perverted
by a wrong concept of liberty and equality (24:172); such a swindle
would have dire consequences. Herder opts for a society that en-
courages the best and discourages the mob. Freedom means to shoulder one's responsibilities, not to do as one pleases. Herder falls back
on Greek aristocratic ideals in his horror of mediocrity and chaos.
With hindsight, it has become clear that controls are almost never
in the right hands, and "positive" versus "negative" ideologies are
most dangerous concepts and weapons. It would be surprising if a
Herder of today would recommend the same controls. The "Atlantis" section nevertheless makes clear that Herder speaks as an
eighteenth-century reformer wary of nineteenth-century liberalism.
Herder, like all his contemporaries, was in favor of *das Volk*, but
afraid of *der Pöbel*. As *das Volk* could not yet act for itself, due to
the unfortunate circumstances, the educated classes were called upon
to shoulder the burden of responsibility.

In the sixth, posthumous, volume of *Adrastea*, Herder returns
once more to the concept of *Nemesis*. This time he finds it in epic
poetry. Homer is not only one of the great poets, but also provided
principles for the writing of history. Homer, in Herder's view, is
one of the main sources for the writing of history. Homer's epics
deal with the confrontation of humans and much stronger invisible
powers. Human beings become heroes fighting such invisible powers. Sometimes, men rebel beyond a permissible measure and are
punished for their hubris. Sometimes, the connections between action and punishment are not quite apparent. The measure of justice,
however, emerges as the rule for all events. This is the principle of
world history that Herder finds exemplified in the work of the
ancient historians. This regard for the right measure, truth, tolerance, and humanity is what Herder demands of modern historians
as well; he finds most of them wanting.

Since it is an orientation in time, historiography becomes part of
history itself. It is an essential part of the educational process deemed
necessary for an improvement of mankind. This process was still at
a stage, Herder maintained (together with many of his contempo-

raries), when democracy was not yet possible. Liberty and equality, while laudable ideals in themselves, cannot be mandated. They are the result of an educational process. Equal rights do not create equal virtues and a communal spirit. Of course, Herder was writing at a time when the negative consequences of unrestrained liberty had caused a mood favoring restrictions. He was at times very much the enlightened educator with a limited amount of patience. He may have been frustrated that he had not been able to make a stronger mark on history as the reformer he wanted to be. At this point, however, Herder was fighting against the tide of history that he had helped to usher in.

Adrastea is not the crowning achievement of a great career. Certain sections betray a lack of concentration. The book still contains important samples of historical writing, especially in the area of literature. Herder's insights are as acute as ever. His principle of nemesis brings with it a largely dialectical view of history not fettered by a rigid system. While his liberal views remain unchanged, he looks for help against the chaos of the age and finds it in delegated state authority. There are dark shadows in Herder's last picture of history, and much less confidence than in the *Ideas.* He was no longer sure whether he should welcome the new century.

Chapter Six
Herder's Many Activities
Herder as a Reviewer

Herder considered the spirit of his age dominated by *Kritik,* and he himself was very much part of it. While he condemned the spirit of *Kritik,* he was a foremost representative of it. It would not be sufficient to differentiate between constructive critique and negative criticism, however. Herder was most concerned about the flood of books in which the really important ideas would be drowned out by ephemeral writing. He always remained ambivalent toward too much reading, although he was a learned man; he was afraid that the truly great books and real life might be forgotten in this deluge of paper. However, a good part of Herder's work could be called extended reviews: Herder was inspired by reading. He was an important critic and he wanted the critic to enter into the spirit of the work under review and evaluate it on the basis of its own premises and stated goals. Criticism, he felt, should be constructive. The ideal critic would be a member of a tribunal that could tell the nation how to make a valid choice among the many books available. Mindful of his own limitations, he wanted to err rather on the positive than on the negative side. He went through different stages, though, in the course of his long career. In addition to his books with their many critiques of other books, Herder wrote a fairly large number of reviews for various journals. Most of them are brief, and some were written in haste. Nevertheless, they merit a brief discussion.

In 1764, Herder's friend Hamann assumed the editorship of the *Königsberger Gelehrten und Politischen Zeitungen.* He urged his young friend to contribute, but Herder was at first hesitant. In 1765 and 1766, however, he became a regular reviewer and wrote at least twenty-eight pieces for the journal. The reviews are perceptive and a clear indication of Herder's interests. He writes on the dithyrambs of Willamovius, on Mallet's history of Denmark, on Thomas Abbt, Dusch's letters on didactic poems, and Kant's *Träume eines Geister-*

sehers. His writing is vivid; he selects works from the areas of poetry, history, and theology. He can be sharp in his criticism when he thinks the work is bad.

Friedrich Nicolai was always looking for reviewers for the *Allgemeine Deutsche Bibliothek* he had started in 1765. He liked Herder's *Fragments* and asked him to contribute. Between 1767 and 1774 Herder must have contributed close to forty reviews to the journal. It has been difficult for literary historians to accept this long collaboration by the champion of the Enlightenment, Nicolai, and the mastermind of *Sturm und Drang,* Herder. But the men did not perceive it in the same manner, and the break between them in 1774 was as much personal as it was "ideological." Nicolai was reluctant to let Herder go. Herder reviewed mostly in the area of poetry and aesthetics; several reviews of Klopstock are especially significant.[1] Herder must have been considered an expert on didactic and other types of reflective poetry. His best known review from this group may be that on Gerstenberg's *Ugolino* of 1768.

Herder also contributed some reviews to the *Wandsbeker Bote* edited by his friend Matthias Claudius,[2] and in 1772 he was involved in Goethe's year of the *Frankfurter Gelehrten Anzeigen,* one of the foremost manifestations of *Sturm und Drang,* where reviews were generally anonymous; yet some reviewers were recognized by their style and occasionally names were leaked. Free to engage in polemics, Herder sometimes went beyond the just measure, mostly in the *Frankfurter Gelehrten Anzeigen,* where his negative review of Schlözer's plan for a *Universal-Historie* had an unpleasant aftermath.[3] The Frankfurt reviews include more theology than other series of reviews, since Herder was able to pick the books himself. There is not much difference in the style of the reviews from the Bückeburg years for the different journals, at most a difference in degree. Contrary to the policy of the *Allgemeine Deutsche Bibliothek,* Herder was not content with a mere summary of the book under review. He spiced his accounts with subjective, often emotional, commentaries. One should still refrain from the term *Erlebniskritik,* however.[4] Reviewing took many shapes and forms during those days, and Herder may have been an innovator less because of subjective emotionalism than for his tendency to develop reviews into short essays. Thus the Ossian essay in *Of German Kind and Art* developed from a review, and the later review of Forster's *Sakuntala* translation provides a prime example.

Between 1776 and 1778, Herder contributed a number of reviews for the *Auserlesene Bibliothek der neuesten deutschen Literatur* in Lemgo. Most of the works reviewed are theological, the reviews of Lavater's works being especially important. Herder supported Lavater's work on physiognomics to which he contributed, for example, a lively characterization of Hamann (*SW*, 9:471–72). These reviews show Herder's closeness to Lavater and his ongoing preoccupation with religious questions.

While Herder continued to comment on books in his *Letters Concerning the Study of Theology*, and again in all of his late works, the review journal in Jena, the *Allgemeine Literaturzeitung*, became Herder's enemy after Kant's review of the *Ideas*. In his *Letters for the Advancement of Humanity*, Herder returned once more to a discussion of the principles of *Kritik*. The Germans ought to be good critics, he feels, because they have common sense, are thorough, and have the courage to be frank (*SW*, 18:125–26). *Kritik* has made real progress from Leibniz to Lessing. In keeping with the character of the Germans, *Kritik* ought to be educational, supportive, with a positive spirit, and humane (18:132). The Germans still need encouragement and respect; they can destroy themselves by negative criticism and unnecessary feuds. While pretending to be unfamiliar with criticism after Lessing's *Literaturbriefe* (17:130)—he himself was one of the most prominent critics, though—he criticizes recent criticism as too partisan and negative, even parochial. England has much more congenial and supportive writings on literature. A genius, he still feels, can only be judged and taught by a genius (18:131). No critic can be a valid judge and guide without some creative abilities and experiences.

Herder had one more opportunity to translate his principles of benevolence and congeniality into practice. The *Akademie nützlicher Wissenschaften* in Erfurt reconstituted its journal under the directives of his friend Karl Theodor von Dalberg (1744–1817), then the *Koadjutor* for the Erfurt area of the archbishopric of Mainz. These reviews in the *Nachrichten von gelehrten Sachen* were signed by the reviewers, a fundamental change that Herder had advocated in the name of responsible criticism. Between 1797 and 1800, Herder wrote at least twenty-six reviews for these *Nachrichten*. The vast majority are educational, supportive, kind, and humane. A curious thing happened in one of the rare exceptions: Herder had cut to pieces a *Geschichte der Religionsschwärmerey*, a history of heretical enthusiastic Christians, by a man named Duttenhofer. In his opinion, it was derivative, copied from other sources, and unnecessary because Duttenhofer's sources were readily available (*SW*, 20:277–82). Duttenhofer protested vigorously, and Herder printed this reply instead of his own review of the second volume which would have been similar to that of the first (20:295–99). Herder wrote on poetry, history, aesthetics, religion, and biography. A particularly sympathetic review was devoted to the Propertius translations of Herder's friend Knebel (20:345–52). A rare example of Herder's interest in the young generation is the review of Sophie Mereau's poems (20:562–67). He emphasized the femininity of the author and is favorably impressed that the poems deal with feminine topics in a proper feminine spirit. His attitude is benevolent although slightly paternalistic. It is still regrettable that he was cut off from the circle of the young writers in Jena.

Herder's reviews are usually well informed and fair. Apart from some forays in the *Frankfurter Gelehrten Anzeigen,* he tried to be kind rather than harsh. His commentaries are relevant, and he clearly sees his review work as part of the work of public enlightenment. Few of the reviews are notable—as Schiller's review on Bürger, Jean Paul's on Madame de Staël, and Goethe's on Johann Heinrich Voss. The *Ugolino* and *Sakuntala* reviews and possibly those on Klopstock may be the most memorable. Herder usually needed more room for a real critique. It is difficult to gain an idea of Herder's preoccupations from such reviews alone. For many years in Weimar, he was not associated with a journal. In his reviews on poetry, his penchant for didacticism is clearly visible. He hardly ever reviewed poetry written by the younger generation after Klopstock.

Herder wrote mostly for journals intended for an educated audience. He wrote in a manner, however, that would open up the world of books for new groups. He liked also to relate books to life in these reviews. He thus expands the language of criticism, although it would be wrong to call him a bold innovator.[5] Herder's reviews are interesting, but they are clearly a by-product. They reflect his personality, but they are a confining medium for him.

Herder as a Translator

When Herder reviewed Knebel's Propertius, he distinguished two kinds of translators: those who translate word for word, and even

may try to find words with the most similar sounds, and those who
re-create a poem as the author would have written it if he had used
the other language (*SW, 20:345*). These two methods seem the only
consistent ones for translating poetry. The first method would be
suitable for interlinear or bilingual editions where the translation
merely helps to gain access to the original. The second method has
been called *Übertragung* or *Nachdichtung,* in contrast to mere *Übersetzung,* and that is certainly what Herder had in mind when he was
translating. He is recognized as a congenial *Nachdichter* who trans-
ferred the spirit and style of the original as a whole without bothering
about word-for-word accuracy.[6] Germans who pride themselves on
the extent and quality of translations of world literature into German
have followed Herder in this tradition of *Nachdichtung. Nachdichtung*
becomes something like an original text that can be enjoyed without
reference to the original. In this manner Johann Heinrich Voss
appropriated Homer and the romantic poets appropriated Shakespeare and Cervantes for German cultural life. The prime example
for any such creative translation remains, of course, Luther's translation of the Bible. At the same time, the many theological questions
raised by Bible translation make it evident that much more than
stylistic issues are involved. The antidogmatism of Herder's generation is very much in accord with moving from the letter to the
spirit of a text, even in translations.[7] Translation was the order of
the day in an age of dramatic reorientation from Latin and French
models to Greek, English, Nordic, Spanish, and Oriental literature.
Herder's new historical awareness also raised the first concerns for
a diachronic dimension of translations. Was it right to modernize
texts from previous ages, or should one try to keep a historical
flavor? Herder made the first steps toward such preservation of
archaic forms, although he wrote distinctly for his contemporaries.

As Herder had stated in his early *Fragments,* translations should
be made to enrich German culture and literature for the purpose of
providing variety and new sources of ideas. Herder remained true
to this goal. He not only gave examples of very successful *Nachdichtungen* himself, but encouraged many others to follow suit. His
most momentous enterprise was undoubtedly his collection of folk
songs. Next to it one needs to mention his *Cid,* running into
numerous editions during the nineteenth century.[8] While they ov-
ershadow Herder's other translations in their reception, he labored
with equal care on many other translations. He was particularly

fond of the work of Jakob Balde (1603 or 1604–68), a Jesuit who wrote in Latin, and whose poems in translation Herder published under the name of *Terpsichore* (1795–96). Herder equally loved Oriental tales and poems, and the Greek *Anthology*. He also translated English poetry of the eighteenth century, Latin poetry, and prose texts like Hemsterhuis's French dialogues.

Herder loved translation. It stimulated his own stylistic powers. He was adaptable and flexible with very diverse styles and rhythmic patterns. While he expertly handled various meters and rhythms, he obviously was not so adroit with rhymes and preferred poetry without rhymes. The foreign original challenged his musical sensibility, his cultural intuition, and his linguistic capabilities. Even some of his own poems may be called adaptations. The line between translation, adaptation, and original creation is not always distinct in his case. Jean Paul Richter characterized Herder as "feminine," meaning that he adapted rather than creating something new; Jean Paul also called Herder a "poem" rather than a "poet."[9] Herder was a mediator, a medium almost, filtering the Greek, Oriental, or primitive world and rendering them familiar. This uncanny talent of intuition and adaptation also indicates his limits. Goethe diagnosed dilettantism to be a foremost problem of his age.[10] In many of his activities Herder was a dilettante in both the good and the bad sense of the word. Most of all, Herder was not a genius as an original poet. He was a great man, but his real creative powers were elsewhere. The limits imposed on his activities in real life may have concentrated his powers more on literary work than his nature really demanded.

Be that as it may, Herder's role as a mediator of foreign worlds was crucial. This is, first of all, true for his collection of folk songs. In 1774, he had brought together a book of English and German songs, but after printing had begun he withdrew the work. After urging from friends, he finally brought out two volumes of *Volkslieder* in 1778 and 1779. For Herder, everything that was genuine and expressed in a natural manner the concerns of common people— life and death, love, jealousy, parting, wedding, work, war, the changing of the seasons, a mother's love for her child, ballads of extraordinary events—could be called folk song, whether or not the author was from the lower classes, and whether or not the song was by an author known by name. The subsequent technical definitions of folk song were foreign to Herder's way of thinking. He included

Goethe's *Heidenröslein,* Claudius's *Abendlied,* and quite a few pieces
from Shakespeare. His collection contains many "real" folk songs
from all over the world, but also some rather artificial and sophisticated songs or lyrical ballads. Herder was certain of a negative
reception, and Karoline virtually had to force his hand. Herder not
only expected misunderstandings from the audience, he also felt
ambivalent about the value of these songs. As it turned out, the
reception was very gratifying. He continued to collect and translate
folk songs; but he died before a third volume was ready. In the
posthumous edition, Karoline gave them the title *Stimmen der Völker
in Liedern* (Voices of the people in songs) and thus provided a label
that has stuck to Herder's enterprise. Herder's thinking was simpler,
less pretentious. He simply gave examples of the poetic expression
of the popular spirit in the world. At the same time, he demonstrated
his philosophy of unity in diversity: these songs express the common
humanity, as well as cultural differences, of mankind. In Herder's
presentation the unity comes through more forcefully than the diversity. With all its variety, the collection bears a specifically Herderian tone, the one in which the next generations received the
concept of style of folk poetry. Herder not only helped to create a
fashion, but he helped to determine the lyrical style of the future.

Herder's interest in the *Cid* romances is evident: they were epic,
narrative ballads dealing with a historical content. Here was the
epic and poetic history that Herder loved. He also felt an affinity
for the exotic medieval Spain of Arabs and Spaniards that was just
being discovered by the Germans. Herder's *Cid* can hardly be called
a "translation." He used different French and Spanish sources and
selected the parts that would make a unified and coherent story.
With his less than adequate knowledge of Spanish he did not always
grasp the exact meanings of idioms of past centuries. Considered
from the point of view of philological accuracy and as a documentation of older Spanish poetry, Herder's *Cid* is the work of a dilettante. But Herder clearly declared his purpose, presenting the "history
of Don Ruy Diaz, count of Vivar" adapted from Spanish romances
(Nach Spanischen Romanzen). Herder wrote a new epic poem in Spanish verse form, adapted and selected from old Spanish poems, partly
through the medium of a French prose translation. When Karoline
changed the above phrase to "nach Spanischen Romanzen besun-
gen," she intimated a much closer relationship to the Spanish orig-

inals than Herder ever intended. Since the new philological sciences were in such vigor during the nineteenth century, and the *Cid* was so popular, much effort was spent on comparing Herder's text with the original Spanish romances, until the crucial importance of the French translation became evident. Herder had translated the Spanish spirit into German and created a poetic history of ancient Spain, but his intuition went beyond his actual knowledge of language and history. Still, the use of Spanish forms in German poetry was encouraged by this work, and the new image of Spain was formed by the *Cid*, together with Tieck's translation of *Don Quijote,* and Schlegel's renderings of Calderón's plays.

Herder also wrote more genuine translations. In Jakob Balde he rediscovered one of the last genuine poets of neo-Latin poetry. Balde would never become as popular as folk songs, Shakespeare, or the *Cid*. But if even these odes are for smaller circles—whether in the original Latin or in Herder's German—they are certainly delightful and vivid. Herder liked these controlled rhythms and this restrained rhetoric; he may have made the odes even more classical than they really were, stressing naturalness and humanity rather than baroque rhetoric. Herder was sympathetic to the content of the poems as well: the complaint about the interminable wars, feeling alien in one's environment, and being homesick for a milder climate.

Herder's translations from Greek poetry show his predilection for didactic and epigrammatic forms. Herder's Oriental legends, fables, and poems are equally didactic. Again, these Oriental works are adapted rather than translated. The Orient presented is very Herderian. Herder strove for an East-West synthesis before Goethe made it a catch word. The accuracy of Herder's translation varies greatly with his degree of knowledge of the original language. However, accuracy was one of the least of his worries; and he was often carried away by the music of poetry, and by his delight for poetry and by its rhythms, tones, forms, and images. He really wanted to be a re-creator and did not feel badly when he passed the line from re-creation to creation. His most important aim was to create a genuine German poem. While keeping the amount of foreign flavor needed for a translation, he created poems that could be enjoyed without any regard to the original. His successors may have surpassed him in accuracy, but Herder had further-reaching aims. He wanted to integrate new modes of expression into German poetry and prose, and he did succeed, most of all with his folk songs and "Spanish" style, but also with Oriental flavor, and with various forms of reflective poetry.

Herder as a Poet

In the thirty-three-volume Suphan edition only two volumes are devoted to Herder's own poetic works: one volume to lyric poetry, one volume to dramatic and narrative forms. This is a minor part of his oeuvre. It has attracted attention mainly for historical reasons: Herder's place in the history of the fable, of the cantata, of the religious legend, of the church song, of the didactic poem.[11] Little interpretative effort has been wasted on Herder's poetic output apart from genre studies. At best, the poems have been used for an elucidation of Herder's religious ideas or his "inner" biography.[12] Indeed, one is tempted to compare Herder's poetic works to those of Goethe, Schiller, Klopstock, and Hölderlin, which are far superior—and thus they pale by comparison. Much of Herder's production is *Gelegenheitsdichtung* (occasional pieces) or "applied" art; he also used genres whose popularity has since vanished. In Herder's latest works, a gap between ambition and achievement is apparent. His real creative powers came to the fore in adaptations and translations rather than in original poetic works. Even in his "original" works, Herder did not invent new plots. He used well-known mythological or historical material. The dividing line between "originals" and adaptations is not clear, not even to editors of Herder's works. Suphan included the *Cid* with the "original" works.

Few of Herder's poems were published during his lifetime. He had given some to Matthias Claudius for the *Wandsbeker Bote,* published others in Boie's *Deutsche Museum* and Wieland's *Teutscher Merkur,* and only toward the end of his life, in a misguided spirit of competition with Goethe and Schiller, offered more poems for Schiller's *Horen* and *Musenalmanache,* and also included them in his *Scattered Leaves,* the *Letters for the Advancement of Humanity,* and *Adrastea.* Herder would probably have made editorial changes if he had ever published an independent volume of poems. As it was, he kept them in nice handwriting in extra volumes for himself and his family and friends.

Herder's early poems followed closely the example of Klopstock. He wrote odes to the czar and the czarine, poems for the wedding of friends in Riga, an ode on the fire that devastated major parts of Königsberg, and an ode to Hamann on the occasion of Herder's departure from Königsberg. His real ambition was as an author of didactic poems, and he was more sure of himself in the grand and the philosophical style than in graceful social pieces. His contributions to the *Wandsbeker Bote* were simple and natural. He never lost his early fondness for epigrammatic forms and fables. His epigrams are not as witty as those of Lessing; they are, however, well phrased, friendly, even witty pieces among them. Some unpublished poems betray his Swiftian vein; the biting tongue was reserved for his close friends. He rarely tried to write ballads or songs in the manner of folk songs. Few nature poems are present. Herder liked allegorical poems, especially in later years. A good number of the unpublished poems are personal, sometimes confessional in nature. Herder's poetic style was as rhetorical as his prose style, with exclamations, rhetorical questions, dashes, and dialogue and monologue. Herder liked dialogue in longer poems, and sometimes imperceptibly moved from lyric to dramatic forms.

He usually called his poems *Schmierereien* (scribblings). But in these scribblings he was often more spontaneous than in other types of expression. Thus certain poems, while not *Erlebnisdichtung* in the manner of Goethe, can well be called *Bekenntnisdichtung* and have an eminently biographical value.

None of Herder's so-called dramatic works approaches the dimensions of a full-length play. They are not really independent forms, but rather have the character of libretti. In Bückeburg Herder collaborated with Johann Christoph Bach, one of the sons of the great Johann Sebastian, on several oratorios: *Brutus*, a *Pfingstkantate*, and *Der Fremdling auf Golgatha*, which describes a stranger witnessing the death of Jesus. He also collaborated with Ernst Wilhelm Wolf in Weimar, for whose 1780 performance of Händel's *Messiah* Herder wrote the German text. Whereas all these activities were connected with Herder's church duties, he also wrote some short allegorical plays in his last years: *Aeon und Aeonis*, on the theme of the old and the new age; *Ariadne-Libera, Der entfesselte Prometheus*, and *Admetus Haus*, his version of the Alcestis story. All plays require music or even suggest some oratorio or operatic form. They could be called festive or festival plays. They radiate an optimistic republican spirit. In the context of the French Revolution and Weimar court festivals masterminded by Goethe, Herder's plays emerge as counterproductions, requiring and fostering a republican spirit. Herder's allegories are general but direct. In the case of Prometheus, Pandora is replaced with a genuine gift, "Agathia," *die reine Mensch-lichkeit* (*SW*, 28:350). Prometheus, having suffered enough for his hubris, is now liberated as a changed person, ready to make a wise choice for humanity. Thus he easily sees through the tricks of Hermes, who wants to entice him with Pandora. *Admetus Haus* celebrates the devotion and sacrifice of the wife for her husband. It is a challenge to the plague of the era, egotism. Humanity and happiness can emerge when human beings help each other. Love, and not egotistical self-fulfillment, is the goal of human existence. Also in *Aeon and Aeonis,* which celebrates the principle of Adrastea and the advent of truth and justice, Aeonis becomes "Agape," love, the daughter of Arete, virtue, who will rule in the future.

Herder's plays thus translate his moral and philosophical concerns into social art. He wanted them to be uplifting, public-spirited, and future oriented. They are *Festspiele* and draw on the tradition of the canata, oratorio, monodrama, and allegory. They are didactic literature. Herder's narrative works are less heavy-handed in this respect. In fact, his *Paramythien* and *Legenden,* as well as many of his fables, show him at his best in poetic prose, graceful language, and clear moral messages conveyed in a liberal and humane spirit.

From these few examples, we can deduce that Herder had a new kind of public-minded literature in mind. His idea of the theater tended toward a kind of *Gesamtkunstwerk,* a *Festspiel* employing all the arts to celebrate the communal spirit, just as he envisioned classical Greek theater. He himself could not provide models, but only made suggestions and indicated directions. Whereas Goethe felt that didacticism interfered with aesthetic purity—although he, too, knew, that it was needed for the common people—Herder would have accepted a less pure form with a more direct message. It is curious to note that Herder may have been a better judge of actual audiences, which becomes immediately clear when one thinks of the manner in which Schiller's classical plays were received by German audiences.

Herder's published poetic works corresponded to the taste of the time and were generally well received. They were forgotten when the taste of the audience changed. As some of the genres became obsolete, Herder, the poet, lost his presence. Undeniably, they have their value as personal documents, as part of his inner biography. A true assessment of their value is still outstanding, especially when compared not only to Goethe, but also to minor poets of the time. It would be of interest as well to analyze how Herder tried to apply his concept of literature to his own poetic works.

Herder as a Preacher

Herder disdained too much rhetoric when he was preaching. His voice was not strong, his diction was simple; yet, all accounts say that he never failed to make an impression on his listeners, and that his audience was silent and attentive when he spoke.[13] He not only preached, but also made speeches at the *Gymnasium* in Weimar, and he spoke at private church functions such as confirmations. Herder disliked the many printed sermons of his day and never wanted to print his own. This is a pity, since we have only a very inadequate record of his preaching, which was such an essential part of his activities. The meager selection printed in the Suphan edition can hardly be called representative,[14] and no new edition has been published since.[15] His preaching is rarely mentioned in scholarship.[16]

In Herder's view, *Der Redner Gottes,* as he called the preacher in an early draft (*SW*, 32:3–11), should not be an actor. He should not be a mindless babbler, *Schwätzer,* he should avoid the usual *Predigtton* and disregard the customary structure of a speech or sermon with its conventional parts (32:5).[17] A sermon should not be rhetorical thunder, or a theological treatise, or social speechmaking. The rhetor of God should not thunder against heretics or freethinkers. Instead, he should give a heartwarming blessing and enter into his sermon with an everyday incident, observation, and experience (32:6). If the audience finds this observation interesting and pertinent to their own lives, they will want to be with the speaker. So the preacher can lead them to the presence of God and to devotion (32:7). This devotion should be *Ton der Seele,* not passion or strain (32:7). One might call it a serene awareness of a divine presence. The preacher is close to a teacher, but his teachings should not be dry precepts. He should engrave a *Bild* (image) on the soul of the listener. This image springs from a situation of human life, colored by religion; it thus becomes morality (32:8). This is how a sermon becomes *ein vollständiges Ganzes* (one and whole). The interconnections of the details are crucial. Dead letters or lifeless moral sayings have no meaning, as systematic as they may be; living experiences and images are needed. The preacher cannot tell an audience what to do, but only prepare them for making their own choices. Practicality is of the essence. The audience must be urged to act right, not merely to have pious feelings and thoughts.

This early plan announces Herder's idea of the functions of a preacher, and the appropriate style. It also places high demands on the preacher. He must possess almost poetic powers to evoke such images in the minds of his listeners. Herder wants his preacher to grasp the whole human being—both intellect and feelings—fill the imagination, and still the passions. A sermon should be a moral experience that stimulates the audience to good actions and decisions. Herder transfers Locke's well-known image of the blank tablet of the mind that has to be filled to his situation as a preacher: a preacher fills the minds of people with good images and thus permanently improves their character and spurs them on to good actions. Obviously such influence is easier to obtain through oral communication than through the medium of print. Therefore, a sermon is superior to a printed book. Poetry should be recited rather than read alone. Here is also the basis for Herder's low esteem of theoretical discourse: it does not change people; at best, it can prepare the ground for change. Herder never fails to complete his books or sections of books with uplifting poetic words, transforming theoretical discussion into moral and practical entreaty.

God's rhetor has to set an example himself. The words will fall flat if the preacher does not live what he preaches. All visitors to Herder's house, even those without Jean Paul's enthusiasm, agreed that Herder's presence was commanding and convincing. With all his depressions and self-doubts, his jealousy and biting sarcasms, he was a graceful and serene host and usually rose to the occasion when his moral counsel and help were needed. He was a particularly trusted adviser of women, but also helped many young men who needed direction. There was a harmonious aura around him; he lived the spirit of his beloved music. His life demonstrated that religion should unite, help, and love, and not divide.

His sermons contain many ideas from his other writings. There is a particular emphasis on Jesus Christ's life and on his teachings according to the gospels. Herder stresses the pure religion of Jesus in contrast to the Judaism of the Pharisees and some of the so-called Christians of later ages. God's word should influence people's actions, and if the minister of the church puts them to sleep instead of awakening his audience, what good can he do, Herder asks in his first sermon in Bückeburg? He never fails to bring the Bible stories close to the lives of his audiences.

A court preacher, even Herder, had to discover the fine line that separated opportunist flattery from genuine respect for the ruler and his office. Herder felt strongly about the moral authority of the minister, especially when he was in high office in one of the states of Martin Luther, the cradle of the Reformation. Since religion should be the guiding light for all human activities, the minister had to be concerned with the entire human life. The limits to which he stretched his moral authority on the basis of such a high regard for his office can be seen in his sermon on the occasion of the birth of a prince and successor to Karl August in 1783. In this sermon (*SW*, 31:520–35), delivered in the presence of the duke, who usually did not attend church services, Herder presented a vivid picture of what he expected from a ruler. He wished the young prince health and a dynamic and happy life, wisdom and insight to rule his people well, and justice and goodness, but also a sense of religion, reverence for God and Jesus Christ, and love for mankind. Rulers, these "gods of the earth," especially needed such love and reverence (*SW*, 31:533). Goethe felt that such implied criticism of Karl August was too harsh. Anna Amalia, the duchess mother, considered the sermon too serious for the occasion; Karl August denied that there were any allusions to himself and wondered how anyone could expect so much from a mere baby—that, at least, is the report Herder received from Wieland and communicated to Hamann in his letter of 19 March 1783 (*Br*, 4:258–59). Herder was keenly aware of the distance between the ideal and the real world. He bemoaned the fact that he had so little influence on the duke, who rarely sought his advice, and then strictly in matters of church administration or education.

Some of Herder's sermons are highly personal. A case in point is his farewell speech in Bückeburg, delivered soon after the death of the countess Maria, who had been close to him. Herder looks back on his five years in Bückeburg and feels that he has achieved nothing. His years there were a complete failure. He admits that he was spoiled by his early success in Königsberg and Riga, and that this failure may have been healthy for him. Thus he scrupulously examines his own shortcomings and those of the others who never accepted him. He tries to see the good side since it made him think about himself and reexamine his priorities and moral standing.

Bückeburg has taught him to go his own way independently of success. After this experience of failure and rejection Herder feels a better Christian and human being, as he says in his final blessing. Herder's sermons are conceived as a direct communication with his audience. He does not lose time with empty phrases and he does not talk up or down. He is involved as a person and strives for the earnest fulfillment of his God-given office. Herder liked preaching and was comfortable addressing audiences. With all his unfeigned humility, he was inspired by the responsibilities of his office, and this colors his speeches and his writings. For many nineteenth-century Germans, the literature and philosophy of the age of Goethe became a substitute religion. Herder's stance was the exact opposite: literature was ultimately at the service of religion—not at the service of a church or a state, but at the service of religion for the advancement of humanity. Herder, the preacher, fights once more against two enemies: narrow orthodoxy and antireligious secularization. Too often only one aspect of his fight is noticed. Herder's sermons confirm his image as a humanistic Christian. He felt the heavy responsibility to carry on Christ's tradition of living faith in a broad-minded and human fashion, preaching universal love in a world full of hatred.

Herder and His Contemporaries

Herder was a major figure in an extremely creative age. He knew most of the prominent figures of German cultural life. It would have been fascinating to have Herder's view of his age in the form of an autobiography. But Herder would have had to live much longer and to be much more detached to be able to be a better judge of himself and others than he was in his last years.

Herder does not fit well among the labels of literary history. Received opinion has it that the Enlightenment was replaced around 1770 by Storm and Stress. At a less certain date, this turned into *Klassik,* to be succeeded by romanticism that began about 1798 with the young generation of the day. Herder seems closest to the Storm and Stress, especially in his Bückeburg writings; and there are real affinities to Goethe after Storm and Stress and before the real *Klassik.* However, in this scheme Herder was out of tune with the time in the 1790s, reverting to Enlightenment ideas and values at the time of *Klassik* and budding romanticism. He was a forerunner of great movements who could not keep up with his followers. This makes him almost a tragic figure. Herder's last publications were not always *erfreulich*, to use Goethe's term. Frustration and constraint were major problems in the last decade of Herder's life. The hostilities of his last years have colored his reception. Goethe did not reveal the full extent of his indebtedness to Herder, and the romantics praised Lessing and Goethe while burying Herder in silence. Jean Paul Richter's moving eulogy after Herder's death could not break this wall of silence. Since Kant and Goethe have been focal points of German cultural history for so long, the reception of Herder had to be ambiguous. Lately, the notion of *Klassik* has been scrutinized more closely,[18] the limitations of Schiller's "aesthetic education" have become more apparent, and it is easier to acknowledge the surprising continuity in Herder's work and thought, especially the elements of the Enlightenment attitude. However, as this book has tried to show, Herder was aware of the dramatic transitions of his age. While he was an innovator and forerunner in many areas, he also saw dangers and was always trying to find a middle ground between two extremes, the just measure and balance. It is easy to see only one side of his struggles.

Herder's difficult and often contradictory personality was, in spite of everything, marked for friendship. He exerted attraction on others, and he was immensely loyal. His first and fundamental friendship was that with Hamann. Herder owed basic ideas to Hamann: that poetry was the mother-tongue of mankind, his concept of the *logos* (the identity of language and reason), a new understanding of the Bible, and his knowledge of Shakespeare. Herder considered Hamann his superior and minimized their differences, so that "Hamann and Herder" became a twin formula for antirationalist thought. However, it is easy to see that Herder's idea of *Humanität* is fundamentally different from Hamann's conception of mankind, and Herder never imitated Hamann's cryptic and aphoristic style. Neither did Herder fight the same fights against the Enlightenment that Hamann was pursuing.[19] Herder admired no one more than Hamann, but he was different. Hamann, the first real mentor of this lonely and shy young man, remained Herder's preferred addressee of letters; no other correspondence covers such a long period in Herder's life. It was fortunate that most of the time their friendship was confined to letters. Thus the sharp disagreement and embarrassed silence over Herder's *Treatise on the Origin of Language* could

be patched up. Hamann published little and might have been overlooked without Herder telling his friends about him. Strangely,
after the praise in the early *Fragments*, Herder never wrote on Hamann, although some quotations and allusions prove that he kept
Hamann's works in mind.[20] It would have been useful to have
Herder's commentary on some of Hamann's work.
    Hamann's influence on Herder was never exclusive, even in Kön-
igsberg. Herder was also Kant's student. He shared Kant's enthusiasm for Rousseau, he imitated Klopstock in poetry, and he was
soon to discover his affinity with Lessing. Kant was then living
under difficult conditions, since he had not yet obtained a professorship. This was an advantage for Herder, because Kant was forced
to lecture on many subjects. He was an inspiring lecturer and a well
meaning teacher, and a good host when he could afford it. Kant,
who never traveled, introduced Herder to geography and astronomy.
Herder's interest in science was stimulated by Kant's *General Natural
History of the Heavens,* and by Kant's lectures, which drew connections
between science, moral philosophy, and metaphysics. Kant was still
searching for his own way: he drew on observation and experience
and invited his students to think for themselves. Herder gained
from Kant's pre-critical period his open and independent attitude,
and his generally empiricist, if not sensualist, outlook. Kant, however, impressed his view on his student Herder that the structure
of the human mind shapes human experience, that the world is not
given, but takes the form of our own experience. In contrast to the
Kantians, who considered the *Critique of Pure Reason* a sacred book,
Herder, like Hamann, was not in awe of Kant: Kant was their friend
and equal, although admired as a great mind. For Herder, the early
Kant was antidogmatic, open-minded, and constructive, whereas
the later *Critiques* ushered in a new era of dogmatism. The illiberal
climate in neighboring Jena may have caused Herder to be unfair
even to Kant's moral and aesthetic views, which had many things
in common with his own, although differences were obvious here
as well. When Herder was Kant's student, Kant's style seemed the
exact opposite of *Schulphilosophie,* of rigorous systems of abstract
words; but the *Critiques* brought back the same old spirit with new
words. For Herder, Kant regressed into Wolffian pedantry, and
while Kant's early works are examples of good German prose style,
Herder felt that the first *Critique* had done violence to the German
language, and thus to natural thinking. The *Metacritique,* with all

its faults, expresses this commonsense horror of a new world of dangerous abstractions. Herder saw Lessing only once for about two weeks in Hamburg in 1770. Lessing had just concluded his productive but disappointing Hamburg years and was ready to leave for Wollfenbüttel—for even greater disappointments. Herder was still young and hopeful. Lessing had appreciated Herder's *Fragments* and especially the first grove of the *Critical Forests*. They were kindred spirits, although Herder was much more in tune with *Empfindsamkeit* and became close to Matthias Claudius almost immediately while he was in Hamburg. Lessing must have been critical of Herder's books of the Bückeburg period, but he read them attentively, certainly *Another Philosophy*. Herder admired *Emilia Galotti,* and especially *Nathan der Weise* and all of Lessing's late publications. He followed closely and sympathetically Lessing's involvement in theological disputes. Lessing's attitudes, as revealed in his works, drew Herder closer to him. He began to write letters, and Lessing responded. They were on the way to a real friendship when Lessing suddenly died. Klopstock and Lessing were the two contemporary writers who elicited extended commentaries from Herder, and what he had to say on Lessing was both personal and meaningful.[21] Herder wrote on topics which Lessing had treated before him: the history of mankind, the search for a better government, palingenesis, death and transformation, Jesus Christ and his religion, as opposed to church orthodoxy, and the theory and practice of literature. For Herder, Lessing, rather than Goethe or Schiller, was the most important German writer of the age. He argued in his books with Lessing's ideas, he praised his works. It was as if he wanted to continue their dialogue which Lessing's unexpected death had cut off.[22] Again, was Herder "retrograde" when he pointed to an Enlightenment writer as a model for future German drama? He was not the only one looking to Lessing for guidance.[23] Lessing's legacy is as significant as it is complex, and Herder was his first heir.

Herder's relationships were never one-sided. Hamann profited considerably from Herder's writings and letters, even when he disagreed, and Lessing took very seriously what Herder wrote and thought. Little is known of Kant's indebtedness to Herder. He may have always regarded him as a gifted student and thus as his inferior. In most of his relationships, however, Herder was more the giver than the receiver. This is true for the most momentous of them,

Herder's friendship with Goethe. In Strassburg, Herder considered Goethe a talented and interested, but immature young man and showered his provocative ideas on the unprepared mind, enjoying somewhat his perplexities. It is doubtful that Herder recognized Goethe's genius and considered himself his "educator." Goethe, however, felt like Herder's "satellite" until they met again in Weimar.

At that time, Goethe had become the writer of *Werther* fame and was close to the duke. He even became, technically, Herder's superior in the administration. Herder did not take this very well, and Goethe did not take decisive steps to reestablish their friendship. It took seven years before the ice was broken—on Goethe's birthday in 1783. Then followed a decade of mutual trust, cooperation, and support. Herder was a sympathetic reviewer and listener of Goethe's works. Goethe's support was vital for Herder's *Ideas*. They were both interested in the natural sciences and worked for the betterment of social conditions in Sachsen-Weimar. Goethe helped to moderate Herder's (and Karoline's) rashness. Herder kept Goethe from becoming an aloof administrator and courtier. They admired Spinoza, strove for *Ganzheit,* and believed in the unity of nature and history. But their friendship was not just "political," that is, based on common convictions and interests; they liked each other and liked to be together. Such personal closeness never arose between Goethe and Schiller. The period was, of course, not without problems. Goethe's efforts on behalf of the dukedom of Sachsen-Weimar proved to be largely futile, and he questioned his own future as a writer and painter. His intense relationship with Charlotte von Stein brought added tension, as it brought happiness. Herder, for his part, was never free of gloomy moods. He saw the constraints of his professional situation and felt a growing distance between the ideal world of reform and the real world of pettiness. Still, the sense of achievement and recognition on Herder's part was stronger. It was one of the good periods of his life.

Different explanations have been offered for the end of their friendship. It is clear that the political disagreements after the French Revolution contributed to this break. In spite of their good intentions, tensions mounted. Goethe's alliance with Schiller in 1794 was caused by his isolation. He no longer felt free to communicate new ideas and manuscripts to Herder. Herder, then, felt rejected and excluded because of the Goethe-Schiller friendship. Herder's initial collaboration on *Die Horen* ended with a dispute with Schiller over the social function of literature. The actual "break" between Herder and Goethe occurred in the fall of 1795 when acute disagreements arose about the manner in which the duke should help with the costs for the education of Herder's sons, as he had promised. While Karoline was impetuous and not always tactful, Goethe's letter to her of 20 October 1795 was devastating and proved how important political disagreements had been for this dispute. Relations grew worse after this, especially between Herder and Schiller. Goethe would have liked to restore cordiality at the personal level. Whether the well-known anecdotal exchange about Goethe's play *Die natürliche Tochter* actually took place, as Goethe describes it, cannot be ascertained. Goethe definitely regretted that Herder's life ended without a resumption of their friendship.[24] It was difficult to keep great egos like those of Goethe and Herder from clashing, especially in the environment of small-town gossip typical for Weimar and Jena. But without the acute tension between the new partisan spirit emanating from France, and the rigid defense of the paternalistic German governments, occasional personal disagreements between Herder and Goethe might have remained unimportant.

Herder still respected Goethe's genius more than he allowed himself to say, and Goethe never lost his awareness of how indebted he was to Herder's example and stimulating ideas. With all limitations, this relationship is fundamental to an understanding of the period.

For Jean Paul Richter, who first met Herder in 1796, Herder was the master and he the disciple. Jean Paul had been a Herder enthusiast since his student days, after reading the *Oldest Document*. Jean Paul's *Hesperus*, attractive to female readers, brought him to Weimar. He decided to live there between 1798 and 1800. His enthusiasm encouraged Herder to keep on writing. He was the first critical reader of the *Metacritique*. Herder introduced Jean Paul to Sophocles' tragedies and gave him a new understanding of Shakespeare. Herder's view of beauty, of ancient Greece, and of history permeates *Titan, Flegeljahre,* and the *Vorschule der Aesthetik* (School for aesthetics). It was the anti-*Klassik*-minded Herder who brought Jean Paul close to classical Weimar. While Jean Paul shared much of Herder's criticism of his age, he tried to rise above partisanship, even and especially in *Titan*. Herder had a limited appreciation of humor and was no real fan of *Hesperus,* unlike Wieland. Jean Paul was intent on obtaining Herder's esteem, and he was gratified by

Herder's reaction to the last volumes of *Titan*. *Flegeljahre*, the book of serene humor, really destined for Herder as the ideal reader, appeared only after Herder's death. Jean Paul was still happy about Karoline's reaction: she was one of the few enthusiasts of this great book, which was rejected by most contemporaries.

These are but few of the relationships that constitute the network of Herder's life. It is significant how his life stood under the principle of communication and impact, that is, of *anbilden*. Jean Paul wanted to acquire some of Herder's superior traits. Herder himself may have striven after some of Lessing's qualities. This network of personal relations must, of course, be seen in the framework of an immensely dynamic and creative age, where give and take of ideas was vital to the development of the nation. Whereas Herder's contributions before 1789 are universally recognized, although not always understood, his opposition to dominant trends in the 1790s still waits a fair assessment.

Herder was a man with an extraordinary intuition and sensitivity for cultural, historical, and stylistic values; his own creativity was stimulated by his immersion in others. He was a genius as a mediator: a translator and adaptor in the broadest sense. He was no creative genius like Goethe, Shakespeare, Homer, and he was no philosopher like Plato, Kant, or Hegel. His unique temperament and talent was Herder's joy and plague; he gave a poetic vision of religion and history, but could not write a *Faust*. Another age and country might have allowed Herder to become a social reformer of significance; fate reduced him to sowing seeds for the future. Many of these seeds are bearing fruit, although their origin has been forgotten. Herder's heritage is important, problematic, but very rewarding. Since it has been fused with the German cultural tradition of the last two centuries, it seems imperative to take a Herderian attitude and follow this heritage back to its origins.

Notes and References

Preface

1. Hans Georg Gadamer, *Volk und Geschichte im Denken Herders* (Frankfurt: Klostermann, 1942), 6.

2. Hans Dietrich Irmscher, "Probleme der Herderforschung," *DVJs* 37 (1963):266–317, and "Der handschriftliche Nachlass Herders und seine Neuordnung," *Herder-Studien,* ed. Walter Wiora (Würzburg, 1960), 1–15.

3. Johann Gottfried Herder, *Werke,* 6th rev. ed., ed. Wilhelm Dobbek, 5 vols. (Weimar, 1982).

4. Johann Gottfried Herder, *Briefe: Gesamtausgabe 1763–1803,* ed. Karl-Heinz Hahn et al. (Weimar, 1977–); hereafter cited as *Br.*

5. Rudolf Haym, *Herder: Nach seinen Leben und seinen Werken dargestellt,* Intro. Wolfgang Harich (Berlin, 1954). The introduction is missing in the 1958 edition.

6. Robert T. Clark, *Herder: His Life and Thought* (Berkeley, 1955).

7. Examples are Christian Grawe, *Herders Kulturanthropologie: Die Philosophie der Geschichte der Menschheit im Lichte der modernen Kulturanthropologie* (Bonn: Bouvier, 1967); Robert S. Mayo, *Herder and the Beginnings of Comparative Literature* (Chapel Hill, 1969); George A. Wells, *Herder and After: A Study in the Development of Sociology* (The Hague, 1959); F. W. Paul Lehmann, *Herder in seiner Bedeutung für die Geographie* (Berlin, 1883); and Friedrich von Baerenbach, *Herder als Vorgänger Darwins und der modernen Naturphilosophie* (Berlin: Grieben, 1877).

8. Introduction to Thomas Carlyle, *Leben Schillers,* Johann Wolfgang v. Goethe: *Sämtliche Worke,* Weimarer Ausgabe sec. 1, vol. 42, pt. 1 (Weimar: Böhlau, 1904), p. 189.

9. A good overview of the scholarship in the German Democratic Republic is provided by the contributions to the *Herder-Kolloquium 1978,* ed. Walter Dietze (Weimar, 1980); cf. also Günther Arnold, "Neue Herder-Literatur in der DDR," in *Impulse: Aufsätze, Quellen, Berichte zur deutschen Klassik und Romantik,* ed. Reiner Schlichting (Berlin: Aufbau, 1982), 4:413–58.

10. Several Herder conferences took place in Bückeburg and these proceedings have been published. The impressive Herder conference in Saarbrücken in November 1984 will be published and is bound to have a stimulating effect.

126

JOHANN GOTTFRIED HERDER

11. See especially the studies of Gillies, Wells, Barnard, and Nisbet cited in the bibliography.

12. Beginning in 1978, regular sessions in various meetings have taken place, whose first outcome is *Johann Gottfried Herder: Innovator Through the Ages*, ed. Wulf Koepke in cooperation with Samson B. Knoll (Bonn 1982).

13. The list is in *Herder-Bibliographie*, ed. Gottfried Günther, Albina A. Volgina, and Siegfried Seifert (Berlin: 1978), 199–204.

14. On the concept and its history see Hans J. Haferkorn, "Zur Entstehung der bürgerlich-literarischen Intelligenz und des Schriftstellers in Deutschland zwischen 1750 und 1800," in *Deutsches Bürgertum und literarische Intelligenz* (Stuttgart: Metzler, 1974), 113–275. On Herder's views on writers, see 145–47, 164–65.

Chapter Two

1. Cf. Introduction by Suphan, in *Sämtliche Werke*, ed. Bernhard Suphan et al., 33 vols. (Berlin, 1877–1913), 1:viii. Herder's works are quoted from the Suphan edition and abbreviated *SW*. The letters are quoted from *Br*.

2. *SW*, 17:284–319. Herder expanded and updated it; the late version ends with a plea for respect for the national language and the struggle for a true fatherland, not a state ruled by princes. Such true fatherlands would and should be peaceful and refrain from committing barbarisms like fighting each other in bloody battles (*SW*, 17:319).

3. *SW*, 1:392; see also his letter to Kant of November 1768 (*Br*, 1:120).

4. Cf. Haym, *Herder*, 1:104–6, and *SW*, 32:3–11; see also the discussion below of Herder as a preacher.

5. See the discussion below of Herder as a preacher.

6. Wilhelm Dobbek, *J. G. Herders Humanitätsidee als Ausdruck seines Weltbildes und seiner Persönlichkeit* (Braunschweig, 1949); Samson B. Knoll, "Herder's Concept of Humanität," in *Johann Gottfried Herder*, ed. Koepke, 9–19.

7. Edgar B. Schick, *Metaphorical Organicism in Herder's Early Works: A Study of the Relation of Herder's Literary Idiom to his World-View* (The Hague, 1971); Frederick M. Barnard, *Herder's Social and Political Thought: From Enlightenment to Nationalism* (Oxford, 1964).

8. Hugh B. Nisbet, *Herder and the Philosophy and History of Science* (Cambridge, 1970); see also cf. Schick, *Metaphorical Organicism*, 108–27; Clark, *Herder*, 303–7.

9. Willy Vontobel, *Von Brockes bis Herder: Studien über die Lehrdichter des 18. Jahrhunderts* (Bern: Grunau, 1942), 246–93; Leif Ludwig Albert-

sen, *Das Lehrgedicht. Eine Geschichte der antikisierenden Sachepik in der neueren deutschen Literatur* (Aarhus: Akademisk Bughandel, 1967), 349–55.

10. Wilfried Barner, "Lessing zwischen Bürgerlichkeit und Gelehrtheit," *Bürger und Bürgerlichkeit im Zeitalter der Aufklärung* ed. Rudolf Vierhaus (Heidelberg: Lambert Schneider, 1981), 165–204; cf. also Haferkorn, "Zur Entstehung."

11. Kurt May, *Lessings und Herders kunsttheoretische Gedanken in ihrem Zusammenhang* (Berlin 1923), gives the most balanced view, although he emphasizes the differences more than the common ground. Cf. also Harald Henry, *Herder und Lessing: Umrisse ihrer Beziehung* (Würzburg: Triltsch, 1941).

12. Lessing to Nicolai, 13 April 1769. Cf. *Johann Gottfried Herder im Spiegel seiner Zeitgenossen,* ed. Lutz Richter (Göttingen, 1978), 61.

13. Erdmann Waniek, "Circle, Analogy and Contrast: On Herder's Style of Thought in his *Journal*," in *Johann Gottfried Herder,* ed. Koepke, 64–84.

14. Bruce Kieffer, "Herder's Treatment of Süssmilch's Theory of the Origin of Language in the *Abhandlung über den Ursprung der* Sprache: A Re-evaluation," *Germanic Review* 53 (1978):93–105.

15. Hans Aarsleff, "The Tradition of Condillac: The Problem of the Origin of Language in the Eighteenth Century in the Berlin Academy before Herder," in *Studies in the History of Linguistics,* ed. Dell Hymes (Bloomington: Indiana University Press, 1974), 93–156. Cf. the abundant material offered by Wolfgang Pross, *Johann Gottfried Herder: Abhandlung über den Ursprung der Sprache* (Munich, 1978).

16. *Herder-Bibliographie,* 513–15; Pross, *Johann Gottfried Herder.*

17. Cf. Aarsleff, "The Tradition of Condillac"; on the question of Herder's originality, see James W. Marchand, "Herder: Precursor of Humboldt, Whorf and Modern Language Philosophy," in *Johann Gottfried Herder,* ed. Koepke, 20–21.

18. Clark, *Herder,* 138.

19. Eric A. Blackall, *The Emergence of German as a Literary Language: 1700–1775,* 2d ed. (Ithaca: Cornell University Press, 1978), 451–81.

20. Wilhelm Dobbek, "Die coincidentia oppositorum als Prinzip der Weltdeutung bei J. G. Herder wie in seiner Zeit," in *Herder-Studien,* 16–47.

Chapter Three

1. One of the harshest critics has been Clark, *Herder,* 163–71; German scholars are generally more lenient.

2. Cf. Wulf Koepke, *Erfolglosigkeit: Zum Frühwerk Jean Pauls* (Munich: Fink: 1977), 236, 238–42.

3. To Johann Heinrich Merck, 15 October 1770; *Br*, 1:261–62. Cf. Clark, *Herder*, 166.

4. Thomas Willi, *Herders Beitrag zum Verstehen des Alten Testaments* (Tübingen: Mohr—Siebeck, 1971); Hans-Joachim Krauss, "Herders alttestamentliche Forschungen," in *Bückeburger Gespräche über Johann Gottfried Herder 1971*, ed. Johann Gottfried Maltusch (Bückeburg, 1973), 59–75.

5. A. Leslie Willson, *A Mythical Image: The Ideal of India in German Romanticism* (Durham: Duke University Press, 1964), 49–71.

6. To Hamann, 23 August 1784; *Br*, 5:62.

7. *Herder-Bibliographie*, 457–58.

8. Friedrich Meinecke, *Werke*, vol. 3, *Die Entstehung des Historismus* (Munich, 1963), 358, 386, 431.

9. *Deutsches Fremdwörterbuch* ed. Otto Basler, vol. 3 (Berlin: de Gruyter, 1977), 412–17. The psychological and political meaning is apparent at the beginning of the eighteenth century, but the idea of a sudden, violent change is added by the French Revolution. Herder's usage reflects that very well. Cf. Günther Arnold, "Wandlungen von Herders Revolutionsbegriff," in *Herder-Kolloquium 1978*, 164–72.

10. Richard Fester, *Rousseau und die deutsche Geschichtsphilosophie* (Stuttgart: Göschen, 1890), 42–67, is typical of the traditional understatement of Rousseau's impact on Herder. Recent German Democratic Republic scholarship may have gone too far in the opposite direction. A reevaluation is still in order.

11. F. Barnard, *Herder's Social and Political Thought*, 153–77, surveys some of Herder's influences. Cf. Wilhelm Raimund Beyer, "Die Herder-Verzerrung im Nationalsozialismus" in *Herder-Kolloquium 1978*, 198–205. This area needs further research.

12. *SW*, 5:xxi. Cf. Hans Dietrich Irmscher in his edition of *Von deutscher Art und Kunst* (Stuttgart, 1968), 139–40.

13. Irmscher, "Anmerkungen," 149; *SW*, 5:xviii–xix.

14. The unnamed friend (*SW*, 5:231) is Goethe. Cf. *Von deutscher Art*, ed. Irmscher, 153, n. Herder's initial criticism of the first version of *Götz* gave way to a lasting admiration.

15. Wulf Koepke, "Truth and Revelation: On Herder's Theological Writings," *Johann Gottfried Herder*, 138–56. On Herder as a church administrator in Bückeburg see Brigitte Poschmann, "Herders Tätigkeit als Konsistorialrat und Superintendent in Bückeburg," *Bückeburger Gespräche über Johann Gottfried Herder 1983*, ed. Brigitte Poschmann (Rinteln, 1984), 190–213.

16. Following Herbert Schöffler, *Protestantismus und Literatur*, the issue has been mainly considered under the heading of secularization. Cf. Albrecht Schöne, *Säkularisation als sprachbildende Kraft*, 2d ed. (Göttingen: Vandenhoeck & Ruprecht, 1968), especially the introduction, 7–36.

17. A balanced view is presented, however, by A. Werner in *Realenzyklopädie für protestantische Theologie und Kirche,* vol. 5 (Leipzig: Hinrichs, 1879), 791–96. Herder was a precursor of later trends. He did not found a "school" or "faction" but stayed with the biblical text, and his New Testament exegesis is innovative.

18. Clark, *Herder,* 177–213, describes Herder's later Bückeburg years under this heading.

19. Karl Aner, *Die Theologie der Lessingzeit* (Halle: Niemeyer, 1929), 79–83.

20. Ulrich Faust, *Mythologien und Religionen des Ostens bei Johann Gottfried Herder* (Münster, 1977).

21. *SW,* 9:vii–xi (introduction).

22. *Caroli Magni progenies, principes ceterum belli gloriaeque cupidi, quare folio Regio citius deiecti, quam, quae Chlodovaeum sequebatur, ignaua imbellisque familia?* (*SW,* 5:699–714), written for an unidentified French Academy. Cf. Haym, *Herder,* 1:696–97. Perhaps Rousseau's example was important for these efforts of Herder.

23. In the 1760s demands multiplied to abolish the university system and replace it by other types of institutions. Cf. Helmut Schelsky, *Einsamkeit und Freiheit: Idee und Gestalt der deutschen Universität und ihrer Reformen* (Reinbek: Rowohlt, 1963), 20–47; René König, *Vom Wesen der deutschen Universität* (Darmstadt: Wissenschaftliche Buchgesellschaft, 1970), 22–40; and Charles E. McClelland, *State, Society and University in Germany* (Cambridge: Cambridge University Press, 1980), 34–98.

Chapter Four

1. Beate Monika Dreike, *Herders Naturauffassung in ihrer Beeinflussung durch Leibniz' Philosophie* (Wiesbaden: Steiner, 1973); Clark, *Herder,* 220; Herbert Schöffler, "Johann Gottfried Herder aus Mohrungen," in *Deutscher Geist im 18. Jahrhundert: Essays zur Geistes- und Religionsgeschichte,* 2d ed. (Göttingen: Vandenhoeck & Ruprecht, 1967), 65–85; Haym, *Herder,* 1:700.

2. Franz Koch, *Goethe und Plotin* (Leipzig: Weber, 1925).

3. *Rein denken* (thinking purely) (*SW,* 8:198) is an impossibility for human beings. Herder has Plato's ideas in mind when he says this. Cf. also *Metacritique* (*SW,* 21:17–21).

4. Cf. Barnard, *Herder's Social and Political Thought,* 33–35 on Locke and Herder. Herder praises Berkeley in his *Metacritique* (*SW,* 21:149, 163–64, 302); he considers Berkeley the real source for David Hume's ideas. The only English writer associated with Herder is usually Shaftesbury.

5. Wulf Koepke, "Herders Totengespräch mit Lessing," in *Auf-*

nahme—Weitergabe: Literarische Impulse um Lessing und Goethe: Festschrift für Heinz Moenkemeyer, ed, John A. McCarthy and Albert A. Kipa (Hamburg: Bluske, 1982), 125–26; and Herder's letters to Lessing, in *Br,* 4:73–74; 93–94, 114–115, 159, 162.

6. Koepke, "Herders Totengespräch mit Lessing," 125–42.

7. Isaiah Berlin, *Vico and Herder: Two Studies in the History of Ideas* (London: Hogarth Press, 1976), on Herder's knowledge of Vico, direct or indirect, 147–48; cf. *Herder-Bibliographie,* 375–76 on other studies, especially by Clark, Erich Auerbach, and George A. Wells. An earlier knowledge of Vico by Herder than has been documented must be assumed.

8. Charles Singer, *A History of Biology: A General Introduction to the Study of Living Things,* 2d ed. (London: Abelard-Schuman, 1959), 218–20 (on Goethe).

9. Willson, *Mythical Image,* 51.

10. Adolf Reichwein, *China and Europe: Intellectual and Artistic Contacts in the Eighteenth Century* (New York: Alfred A. Knopf, 1925), 151, 153; and Ursula Aurich, *China im Spiegel der deutschen Literatur des 18. Jahrhunderts* (Berlin: Ebering, 1935), 39.

11. Rudolf Unger, "Herder und der Palingenesiegedanke," in *Herder, Novalis und Kleist* (Darmstadt: Wissenschaftliche Buchgesellschaft, 1973), 1–23; and Ursula Cillien, *Johann Gottfried Herder: Christlicher Humanismus* (Ratingen 1972), 142–49.

12. Hermann Timm, *Gott und die Freiheit* (Frankfurt: Klostermann, 1974); Martin Bollacher, *Der junge Goethe und Spinoza* (Tübingen: Niemeyer, 1969); and Regine Otto, "Herder auf dem Wege zu Spinoza," *Weimarer Beiträge* 24 (1978):165–77.

13. Emil Adler, "Pantheismus—Humanität—Promethie: Ein Beitrag zur Humanitätsphilosophie Herders," in *Bückeburger Gespräche über Johann Gottfried Herder 1971,* 77–90; and Friedrich Wilhelm Strothmann, "Das scholastische Erbe im Herderschen 'Pantheismus,' " *Dichtung und Volkstum* 37 (1936):174–87. Both contributions discuss diverse aspects of this complex problem.

14. The case of Heinrich Heine is of course most pertinent. But twentieth-century writers would be interesting as well. For Brecht see Otto F. Best, *Bertolt Brecht: Weisheit und Überleben* (Frankfurt Suhrkamp, 1982), 163–72. Lion Feuchtwanger would be a good example.

15. See Herder's letter to Friedrich Heinrich Jacobi of 6 February 1784; *Br,* 5:27–29.

16. Dobbek, "Die coicidentia oppositorum als Prinzip der Weltdeutung bei J. G. Herder wie in seiner Zeit." *Herder-Studien,* 16–47.

17. Haym, *Herder,* 2:319, 327; and Clark, *Herder,* 343–44.

18. Herbert Lindner, *Das Problem des Spinozismus im Schaffen Goethes und Herders* (Weimar: Arion, 1960).

19. Unfortunately, the exaggerated claims of Günther Jacoby, *Herder als Faust* (Leipzig: Meiner, 1911), have stifled research in this area. Interesting parallels are offered by Alexander Gillies, *Herder* (Oxford, 1945), 60–62, 67, 81–86, 99–102, 109–10.

20. For the justification of the principles of the Suphan edition, cf. 16:618. Suphan separated prose and poetry only when Herder inserted whole groups or collections of poems, stories, or other literary texts. Individual poems were left in place. Inevitably, this procedure could not be followed with consistency. In any case, it was against Herder's own intentions.

21. Koepke, "Herders Totengespräch mit Lessing," 125–42.

22. Ludwig Uhlig, *Der Todesgenius in der deutschen Literatur von Winckelmann bis Thomas Mann* (Tübingen: Niemeyer, 1975), 19–29.

23. O. Kirn, "Wiedergeburt," in *Realenzyklopädie für protestantische Theologie und Kirche,* vol. 21 (Leipzig, 1908), 246–56; Cillien, *Christlicher Humanismus.*

24. Willson, *Mythical Image,* 49, 56, 69–71.

Chapter Five

1. Cf. *Herder-Bibliographie,* 355–61, on the abundant literature of the *Humanitätsidee;* see also Edna Purdie, "Some Renderings of Humanitas in German in the Eighteenth Century," in *Studies in German Literature of the Eighteenth Century* (London, 1965), 151–71, especially 156–62.

2. The *Letters* are frequently quoted as "*zur* Beförderung der Humanität," but Herder's title is "*zu* Beförderung . . ."; cf. *SW,* 18:608, n. 1.

3. While the word as such did exist, Herder gave it its characteristic meaning; cf. *Deutsches Wörterbuch,* 1:295.

4. Helmuth Kiesel and Paul Münch, *Gesellschaft und Literatur im 18. Jahrhundert* (Munich: Beck, 1977), 174–79; and Albert R. Schmitt, "Neues zum deutschen Amerikabild: 1775–1777," *Modern Language Notes* 91 (1976):397–423.

5. Cf. *Herder-Bibliographie* 404–5, 520, on the recent and abundant literature on Herder and the French Revolution.

6. Wulf Koepke, ". . .'das Werk einer glücklichen Konstellation': Schillers *Horen* und die deutsche Literaturgeschichte," in *Friedrich Schiller: Kunst, Humanität und Politik in der späten Aufklärung* ed. Wolfgang Wittkowski (Tübingen: Niemeyer, 1982), 378–79.

7. *SW,* 18:540–42 on the *Freitagsgesellschaft* in Weimar.

8. Richard Critchfield, "Revolution and the Creative Arts: Toward a Reappraisal of Herder's Defense of the French Revolution," in *Johann Gottfried Herder,* ed. Koepke, 190–206.

9. Joachim Wohlleben, "Goethes Literaturkritik: Die Wandlungen der Grundeinstellung Goethes als Kritiker von der Rückkehr aus Italien bis zu seinem Tode" (Ph.D. diss., Free University of FU Berlin, 1965), 127–32.

10. The "rehabilitation" of *Kalligone* began with Heinz Begenau's *Grundzüge der Ästhetik Herders* (Weimar: Böhlau, 1956), which was followed by a number of special studies. A close examination of the late Herder in view of recent studies remains to be written.

11. Cillien, *Christlicher Humanismus*.

12. Such questions are revelation, the resurrection of Jesus Christ, and "Von dem Zwecke Jesu und seiner Jünger" (Gotthold Ephraim Lessing, *Werke* [Munich: Hanser, 1976], 7:344–88, 398–457, 496–604).

13. Günther Wirth, "Herder als Theologe," *Herder-Kolloquium 1978*, 259–64, refers to Albert Schweitzer and Karl Barth.

14. *SW*, 17:403–5; the first draft attempted a cautious appraisal of Kant's critical philosophy (18:324–27).

15. Cf. the introduction to *SW*, 21:vi–viii.

16. Luanne Frank, "Herder and the Maturation of Hamann's Metacritical Thought: A Chapter in the Pre-History of the *Metakritik*," *Johann Gottfried Herder*, ed. Koepke, 157–89.

17. Begenau, *Grundzüge;* see also *Herder-Bibliographie*, 538.

18. Haym, *Herder*, 2:714–30, especially 728–30.

19. Dieter Arendt, *Der "poetische Nihilismus" in der Romantik* (Tübingen: Niemeyer, 1972), 1:6, 38.

20. Haym, *Herder*, 2:749; Haym certainly underestimated *Kalligone*.

Chapter Six

1. On Herder's relations to Klopstock, cf. Dieter Lohmeyer, *Herder und Klopstock. Herders Auseinandersetzung mit der Persönlichkeit und dem Werk Klopstocks* (Bad Homburg, 1968).

2. Max Wedel, *Herder als Kritiker* (Berlin: Ebering, 1928), 113–19, tries to identify the reviews by Herder.

3. Haym, *Herder*, 1:635–44.

4. Wedel, *Herder als Kritiker* 33–38, 91–97. If Herder argues in his *Ugolino* review, "We do not criticize from Hedelin, or Racine, but from our feeling" (*SW*, 4:311), he means by "we" the readers or theater audience. See also Anni Carlsson, *Die deutsche Buchkritik* (Stuttgart: Kohlhammer, 1963), 1:68–70.

5. René Wellek, *A History of Modern Criticism: 1750–1950*, vol. 1, *The Later Eighteenth Century* (New Haven, 1955), 181–200, stresses Herder's significance for the history of European literature and criticism, but

he does not deal specifically with the reviews, evidently considering them of minor importance.

6. Ralph-Rainer Wuthenow, *Das fremde Kunstwerk: Aspekte der literarischen Übersetzung* (Göttingen: Vandenhoeck & Ruprecht, 1969), 56–85; Edna Purdie, "Some Problems of Translation in the Eighteenth Century in Germany," in *Studies in German Literature of the Eighteenth Century,* 111–31, especially 123–28; Thomas Huber, *Studien zur Theorie des Übersetzens im Zeitalter der deutschen Aufklärung 1730–1770* (Meisenhain: Anton Hain, 1968), 69–80; Winfrid Sdun, *Probleme und Theorien des Übersetzens in Deutschland vom 18. bis zum 20. Jahrhundert* (Munich: Hueber, 1967), 25–30; Andreas F. Kelletat, *Herder und die Weltliteratur. Zur Geschichte des Übersetzens im 18. Jahrhundert* (Frankfurt; Bern: Peter Lang, 1984).

7. "Literalism" would exclude the interpretation of the Bible as a collection of poetic-historical documents, whose style is determined by their cultural background. Herder's own Bible translations in the *Oldest Document* and the *Spirit of Hebrew Poetry* attempt to make the ancient text accessible to contemporary readers, irrespective of dogmatic consequences.

8. *Herder-Bibliographie,* 100–10. The Cotta edition, which was originally part of Herder's *Works,* ran through seventeen separate printings in the nineteenth century. Thirty-six other editions appeared, some of them reissued several times.

9. Jean Paul Richter, *Werke,* vol. 5, *Vorschule der Aesthetik* (Munich: Hanser, 1965), 451–52.

10. Hans Rudolf Vaget, *Dilettantismus und Meisterschaft: Zum Problem des Dilettantismus bei Goethe; Praxis, Theorie, Zeitkritik* (Munich: Winkler, 1972).

11. Bodo Lecke, *Das Simmungsbild, Musikmetaphorik und Naturgefühl in der dichterischen Prosaskizze 1721–1780* (Göttingen: Vandenhoeck & Ruprecht, 1967), 109–18; Vontobel, *Von Brockes bis Herder;* August Langen, *Dialogisches Spiel: Formen und Wandlungen des Wechselgesanges in der deutschen Dichtung (1600–1900)* (Heidelberg: Winter, 1966); Hellmut Rosenfeld, *Legende* (Stuttgart: Metzler, 1961); F. A. Cunz, *Geschichte des deutschen Kirchenliedes* (Leipzig: Löschke, 1855); August Wünsche, *Die Pflanzenfabel in der Weltliteratur* (Leipzig: Akademischer Verlag für Kunst und Wissenschaft, 1905).

12. Erich Ruprecht, "J. G. Herders Bekenntnisgedichte: Selbstbefragung und Selbstgewissheit," in *Bückeburger Gespräche über Johann Gottfried Herder 1983,* 174–89; see also the succinct discussion of the poems in Joe K. Fugate, *The Psychological Basis of Herder's Aesthetics* (The Hague, 1966), 265–79.

13. *Herder im geistlichen Amt,* ed. Eva Schmidt (Leipzig, 1956), 256–61. This contains documents of contemporary listeners. Karoline mentions several such scenes in her *Erinnerungen.*

14. Irmscher, "Der handschriftliche Nachlass Herders und seine Neuordnung," 10; see also Irmscher, "Probleme der Herderforschung." For a recent discussion of the problem, cf. Wilhelm Ludwig Federlin, *Vom Nutzen des Geistlichen Amtes* (Göttingen: Vandenhoeck & Ruprecht, 1982), who calls for a new assessment of Herder's sermons.

15. In contrast, Herder's *Schulreden* have been included in most editions of his works and have been published in some separate editions.

16. *Herder-Bibliographie,* 294–96.

17. On these conventional parts, see Heinrich Lausberg, *Handbuch der literarischen Rhetorik* (Munich: Hueber, 1980); and "Homiletik und Rhetorik," in *Realenzyklopädie für protestantische Theologie und Kirche,* vol. 6 (Leipzig, 1880), 273–75.

18. Karl Otto Conrady, "Anmerkungen zum Konzept der Klassik," in *Deutsche Literatur zur Zeit der Klassik,* ed. Karl Otto Conrady (Stuttgart: Reclam, 1977); Malsch, "Klassizismus, Klassik und Romantik der Goethezeit," 381–408; *Die Klassik-Legende,* ed. Reinhold Grimm and Jost Hermand (Frankfurt: Athenäum, 1971).

19. Rudolph Unger, *Hamann und die Aufklärung* (Jena: Diederichs, 1911).

20. *SW,* 17:83, 21:290, 22:121, 145, 231; the largest number of quotations occur in *Kalligone.*

21. Henry, *Herder und Lessing.*

22. Koepke, "Herders Totengespräch mit Lessing."

23. Wulf Koepke, "Der späte Lessing und die junge Generation," in *Humanität und Dialog: Lessing und Mendelssohn in neuer Sicht,* ed. Ehrhard Bahr, Edward P. Harris, and James G. Lyon (Detroit: Wayne State University Press, 1979), 211–22.

24. "Herder," in *Biographische Einzelheiten,* J.W.v.Goethe: SW (Weimar: Böhlau, 1893) 36:254–56.

Selected Bibliography

PRIMARY SOURCES

1. German Editions

Sämtliche Werke. Edited by Bernhard Suphan et al. 33 vols. 1877–1913. Reprint. Hildesheim: Georg Olms, 1967. In spite of its flaws, this is the authoritative, and most complete of all editions and as such is indispensable for research.

Werke. Edited by Wilhelm Dobbek. 5 vols. 6th ed. Weimar: Volksverlag, 1982. So far the only post–World War II edition of a representative selection of Herder's work.

Werke. Edited by Wolfgang Pross and Pierre Penisson. 3 vols. Munich: Carl Hanser, 1983–. A selection of Herder's works with introductions and good annotations, not yet complete.

Werke. 10 vols. Frankfurt: Deutscher Klassiker Verlag, 1985–. This edition, which is just beginning to appear, promises to become the most representative edition of select works.

Sprachphilosophische Schriften. Edited by Erich Heintel. Hamburg: Meiner, 1960. Herder's major works on the theory of language.

Abhandlung über den Ursprung der Sprache. Edited by Hans Dietrich Irmscher. Stuttgart: Reclam, 1966.

Abhandlung über den Ursprung der Sprache. Text, Materialien, Kommentar. Edited by Wolfgang Pross. Munich: Carl Hanser, 1978. The commentary and notes are most valuable.

Ideen zur Philosophie der Geschichte der Menschheit. Darmstadt: Melzer, 1966.

Auch eine Philosophie der Geschichte zur Bildung der Menschheit. Edited by Hans-Georg Gadamer. Frankfurt: Suhrkamp, 1967.

Stimmen der Völker in Liedern (Volkslieder). Edited by Christel Käschel. Leipzig: Reclam, 1968.

Stimmen der Völker in Liedern (Volkslieder). Edited by Heinz Rölleke. Stuttgart: Reclam, 1975. Interesting notes.

Von deutscher Art und Kunst. Edited by Hans Dietrich Irmscher. Stuttgart: Reclam, 1968. The handiest edition of the entire volume with the contributions of Herder, Goethe, Frisi, and Möser.

Journal meiner Reise im Jahre 1769. Edited by Katharina Mommsen. Stuttgart: Reclam, 1976. Particularly valuable introduction and notes.

2. Letters, Documents, and Bibliography

Briefe: Gesamtausgabe 1763–1803. Edited by Karl-Heinz Hahn et al. Weimar: Böhlau, 1977–. When completed, this edition (in 9 volumes) will be the first complete collection of Herder's letters.

Briefe. Edited by Wilhelm Dobbek. Weimar: Volksverlag, 1959. A representative selection of 214 letters.

Briefe. Edited by Regine Otto. Weimar: 1970. A selection of 173 letters by Herder.

Erinnerungen aus dem Leben Johann Gottfried von Herders. Edited by Johann Georg Müller. 2 vols. Tübingen: Cotta, 1820. Based on a manuscript of Herder's widow Karoline.

Johann Gottfried von Herders Lebensbild. Edited by Emil Gottfried von Herder. 3 vols. Erlangen: Bläsing, 1846. Mostly letters; selected by one of Herder's sons.

Aus Herders Nachlass. Edited by Heinrich Düntzer and Ferdinand Gottfried von Herder. 3 vols. Frankfurt: Meidinger, 1856–57. Letters from and to Herder.

Von und an Herder. Edited by Heinrich Düntzer and Ferdinand Gottfried von Herder. 3 vols. Leipzig: Dyk, 1861–62. Letters from and to Herder.

Johann Gottfried Herder: Sein Leben in Selbstzeugnissen, Briefen und Berichten. Edited by Hans Reisiger. Berlin: Propyläen-Verlag, 1942.

Johann Gottfried Herder im Spiegel seiner Zeitgenossen: Briefe und Selbstzeugnisse. Edited by Lutz Richter. Göttingen: Vandenhoeck & Ruprecht, 1978.

Herder-Bibliographie. Edited by Gottfried Günther, Albina A. Volgina, and Siegfried Seifert. Berlin: Aufbau, 1978. The most up-to-date and by far the most complete bibliography; an indispensable reference work.

Der Handschriftliche Nachlass Johann Gottfried Herders: Katalog. Edited by Hans Dietrich Irmscher and Emil Adler. Wiesbaden: Harassowitz, 1979. A catalog of Herder manuscripts and unpublished writings.

3. English Editions

Journal of My Travels in the Year 1769. Translated by Francis Harrison. Ph.D. diss., University of South Carolina, 1953.

God, Some Conversations. Translated by Frederick H. Burkhardt. 1940. Reprint. Indianapolis: Bobbs-Merrill, 1962.

Essay on the Origin of Language. Translated by John H. Moran and Alexander Gode. New York: Frederick Ungar, 1967.

Reflections on the Philosophy of the History of Mankind. Chicago: University of Chicago Press, 1968. This is a selection from the translation of the Ideen by T. O. Churchill, *Outlines of a History of Man* (London, 1800).

Yet Another Philosophy of History for the Education of Humanity. Translated by Eva Herzfeld. Ph.D. Diss., Columbia University, 1968.

SECONDARY SOURCES

Adler, Emil. *Herder und die deutsche Aufklärung.* Vienna; Europa, 1968. A fundamental study from a Marxist point of view, presenting Herder in the framework of the Enlightenment.

Barnard, Frederick M. *Herder's Social and Political Thought: From Enlightenment to Nationalism.* Oxford: Clarendon Press, 1965. A well-reasoned approach to Herder's organic thinking and organic politics.

Begenau, Heinz. *Grundzüge der Ästhetik Herders.* Weimar: Böhlau, 1956. Particularly valuable for its reappraisal of the late Herder.

Blackall, Eric A. "The Imprint of Herder's Linguistic Theory on His Early Prose Style." *PMLA* 76 (1961):512–18. Short but significant study of Herder's language theory and style, especially the principle of immediacy.

Cillien, Ursula *Johann Gottfried Herder: Christlicher Humanismus.* Ratingen: A. Henn, 1972. Language, art, religion, and politics viewed under the aspect of *Humanismus* and *Humanität.* Discussion of problems like freedom, evil, nemesis, and palingenesis.

Clark, Robert T. "Herder's Conception of 'Kraft.' " *PMLA* 57 (1942):737–52. A careful analysis of one of Herder's most problematic key concepts.

———. *Herder: His Life and Thoughts.* Berkeley: University of California Press, 1955. The most detailed biography in English, with a "vitalistic bias" and some one-sided evaluations.

Dietze, Walter. *Johann Gottfried Herder: Abriss seines Lebens und Schaffens.* Berlin: Aufbau, 1980. A short biography that stresses social conflicts in Herder's life and the progressive aspects of his work from a Marxist perspective.

———, ed. *Herder-Kolloquium 1978.* Weimar: Harmann Böhlau, 1980. Collection of papers on diverse aspects of philosophy of history, idea of humanity, the *Volk,* and theory of culture and aesthetics; represents recent scholarship in the German Democratic Republic.

Dobbek, Wilhelm. *J. G. Herders Humanitätsidee als Ausdruck seines Weltbildes und seiner Persönlichkeit.* Braunschweig: Georg Westermann, 1949. An examination of the concept of *Humanität,* deriving it from Herder's personality and claiming a central position for it in Herder's world view. Implied is an attempt to refute the image of Herder before 1945.

138   JOHANN GOTTFRIED HERDER

―――. "Herder und Shakespeare. *Shakespeare-Jahrbuch* 91 (1955):25–51.
An examination of Herder's reception of Shakespeare and his contributions to an understanding of Shakespeare in Germany.
―――. *J. G. Herders Weltbild: Versuch einer Deutung.* Cologne: Böhlau,
1969. Examination of key concepts and problems in Herder's works,
in order to demonstrate the underlying unity of his thinking.
Ergang, Robert Reinhold. *Herder and the Foundations of German Nationalism.* 1931. Reprint. New York: Octagon Books, 1966. A thorough
study of Herder's conception of nationality with exaggerations and
some factual errors. Herder is aligned with the wave of German
nationalism after 1807. The book, written before the misuse of Herder
by Nazi Germany, hails nationalism as a great positive trend.
Faust, Ulrich. *Mythologien und Religionen des Ostens bei Johann Gottfried
Herder.* Münster: Aschendorff, 1977. Herder's ideas on Asian religions: their histories and their relationships.
Federlin, Wilhelm Ludwig. *Vom Nutzen des Geistlichen Amtes. Ein Beitrag
zur Interpretation und Rezeption Johann Gottfried Herders.* Göttingen:
Vandenhoeck & Ruprecht, 1982. A thorough discussion of Herder's
vocation as a preacher and its significance for his entire work.
Fugate, Joe K. *The Psychological Basis of Herder's Aesthetics.* The Hague:
Mouton, 1966. A discussion of Herder's aesthetic thought from the
Fragments to *Kalligone,* with sections on Herder's concept of the drama
and on poetry and an evaluation of his poetry.
Gillies, Alexander. "Herder and Faust." *Publications of the English Goethe
Society,* n.s., 16 (1947):90–111. Herder's philosophy, especially from
the *Ideas,* in its influence on the later parts of *Faust.*
―――. *Herder.* Oxford: Blackwell, 1945. A general introduction to Her-
der's life and work with special emphasis on the issue of folk poetry,
the influence of Shakespeare, Herder's impact on Goethe, particularly
Faust, and the philosophy of history in its theological roots.
Haym, Rudolf. *Herder: Nach seinem Leben und seinen Werken dargestellt.* 2
vols. 1877–85. Reprint. Berlin: Aufbau, 1954. After one hundred
years this book remains the fundamental biography and introduction
to Herder's works, in spite of an "antipoetic" bias.
Irmscher, Hans Dietrich. "Johann Gottfried Herder." In *Deutsche Dichter
des 18. Jahrhunderts: Ihr Leben und Werk,* edited by Benno von Wiese,
524–50. Berlin: Erich Schmidt, 1977. A short general introduction
to Herder's life and thought, concentrating on his ideas of literature
and language.
Jäger, Hans-Wolf. *Herder.* In *Neue deutsche Biographie,* 8:595–603. Berlin:
Duncker & Humblot, 1969. A concise dictionary entry with bibliography, stressing the progressive aspects of Herder's life and thought.
Jöns, Dietrich Walter. *Begriff und Problem der historischen Zeit bei Johann*

Gottfried Herder. Stockholm: Almqvist & Wiksell, 1956. An examination of the conception of time, discussing terms like *Zeitalter*, *Zeitgeist*, and the attitude toward history and after life.

Kantzenbach, Friedrich Wilhelm. *Herder in Selbstzeugnissen und Bilddokumenten*. Reinbek: Rowohlt 1970. Useful overview with many quotations and an extensive bibliography.

Koepke, Wulf, ed. *Johann Gottfried Herder: Innovator through the Ages*. Bonn: Bouvier, 1982. Eleven studies by North American scholars; extensive bibliography. Contains new approaches to various Herder problems especially his method of thinking.

Kohlschmidt, Werner. *Herder-Studien: Untersuchungen zu Herders kritischem Stil und zu seinen literaturkritischen Grundeinsichten*. Berlin: Junker & Dünnhaupt, 1929. Still one of the best studies of Herder's style, although it downplays the rational elements.

Kühnemann, Eugen. *Herder*. 2d ed. Munich: Beck, 1912. Stimulating biography, not suitable for reference; many value judgments.

Lohmeier, Dieter. *Herder und Klopstock: Herders Auseinandersetzung mit der Persönlichkeit und dem Werk Klopstocks*. Bad Homburg: Gehlen, 1968. Herder's personal relationship with Klopstock and his reviews and interpretations of Klopstock's works.

McEachran, Frank. *The Life and Philosophy of Johann Gottfried Herder*. Oxford: Clarendon Press, 1939. In spite of the title this is not really a discussion of Herder's philosophy, but an introduction to his life and work, superseded by works like those of Clark and Barnard.

Maltusch, Johann Gottfried, ed. *Bückeburger Gespräche über Johann Gottfried Herder 1971*. Bückeburg: Grimme, 1973.

———, ed. *Bückeburger Gespräche über Johann Gottfried Herder 1975*. Rinteln: Bösendahl, 1976. Two collections (edited by Maltusch) of significant symposium papers of conferences in Bückeburg.

May, Kurt. *Lessings und Herders kunsttheoretische Gedanken in ihrem Zusammenhang*. Berlin: Emil Ebering, 1923. Stresses the differences rather than the similarities, in accordance with the idea of a break between the Enlightenment and Storm and Stress. Yet the interpretations are still useful.

Mayo, Robert S. *Herder and the Beginnings of Comparative Literature*. Chapel Hill: University of North Carolina Press, 1969. Evidence for the claim that Herder was one of the major initiators of comparative literature studies.

Meinecke, Friedrich. *Werke*. Vol. 3, *Die Entstehung des Historismus*. Munich: Oldenbourg, 1959. In his chapter on Herder (355–444), Meinecke claims Herder as the most significant forerunner of Historicism, without denying the eighteenth-century heritage.

Nisbet, Hugh B. *Herder and the Philosophy and History of Science*. Cambridge:

Modern Humanities Research Association, 1970. A detailed examination of Herder's place in the history of the physical, biological,
and social sciences, and an analysis of his philosophy.

Owren, Heidi. *Herders Bildungsprogramm und seine Auswirkungen im 18. und
19. Jahrhundert.* Heidelberg: Carl Winter, 1985. Herder's pedagogical ideas, their realization in his time, and their influence.

Poschmann, Brigitte, ed. *Bückeburger Gespräche über Johann Gottfried Herder
1983.* Rinteln: C. Bösendahl, 1984. Fourteen studies by well-known
scholars that concentrate on the philosophy of history of the earlier
Herder, on Herder's concept of the Reformation and Martin Luther,
and on Herder's official duties in Bückeburg.

Purdie, Edna. *Studies in German Literature of the Eighteenth Century: Some
Aspects of Literary Affiliation.* London: Athlone Press, 1965. Several
articles dealing with Herder's Shakespeare reception and the history
of ideas, for example, the term *Humanität.*

Schick, Edgar B. *Metaphorical Organicism in Herder's Early Works: A Study
of the Relation of Herder's Literary Idiom to His World-View.* The Hague:
Mouton, 1971. This study concentrates on the meaning and significance of the plant metaphors in Herder's works until 1778.

Schmidt, Eva, ed. *Herder im geistlichen Amt: Untersuchungen, Quellen, Dok-
umente* Leipzig: Koehler & Amelang, 1956. A good introduction to
Herder's activities as a minister and church administrator.

Schmitt, Albert R. *Herder und Amerika.* The Hague: Mouton, 1967.
Herder's view of the Americas, his anticolonialism, his enthusiasm
for Benjamin Franklin, and his empathy with the American Indians.

Schöffler, Herbert. "Johann Gottfried Herder aus Mohrungen," In *Deutscher
Geist im 18. Jahrhundert,* 61–85. Göttingen: Vandenhoeck & Ruprecht, 1956. The significance of Herder's Lutheran heritage and his
transformation of Protestant ideas.

Schütze, Martin. "The Fundamental Ideas in Herder's Thought." *Modern
Philology* 18 (1920):67–78, 289–302; 19 (1921):113–30, 361–82;
21 (1923):29–48, 113–32. An examination of key concepts, such as
individualization, personality, spontaneity, the genetic conception,
and living force.

Stahl, Ernst Leopold. *Die religiöse und die humanitätsphilosophische Bildung-
sidee und die Entstehung des deutschen Bildungsromans im 18. Jahrhundert.*
Bern: Paul Haupt, 1934. Thorough discussion of Herder's idea of
Bildung in the context of German intellectual history.

Unger, Rudolf. *Herder, Novalis und Kleist.* Frankfurt: Diesterweg, 1922.
Several studies dealing with Herder's idea of palingenesis and his
influence on the romantics, especially Novalis.

Wellek, René. *A History of Modern Criticism: 1750–1950.* Vol. 1, *The
Later Eighteenth Century.* New Haven: Yale University Press, 1955.

Concise discussion of Herder's position and significance in the history of literary criticism (181–200).

Wells, George A. *Herder and After: A Study in the Development of Sociology.* The Hague: Mouton, 1959. A detailed commentary on the *Ideas* and a critical history of its reception in the nineteenth century, stressing the nonreception of Herder's empiricism.

Wiora, Walter, ed. *Herder-Studien.* Würzburg: Holzner, 1960. A collection of Herder studies. Most important is Wilhelm Dobbek's "Die coincidentia oppositorum als Prinzip der Weltdeutung be J. G. Herder wie in seiner Zeit" (16–47) and H. D. Irmscher's article on Herder's *Nachlass.*

Wolff, Hans M. "Der junge Herder und die Entwicklungsidee Rousseaus," *PMLA* 57 (1942):753–819. The most helpful study of Rousseau and Herder.

Index

DATE DUE

DEMCO 38-297